UPDATED AND REVISED EDITION

THE FLORIDA KEYS
Dive Guide

Text and photographs by
STEPHEN FRINK *and* WILLIAM HARRIGAN

Editing provided by
Diving Science and Technology Corp. (DSAT)
a corporate affiliate of
Professional Association of Diving Instructors (PADI)

ABBEVILLE PRESS PUBLISHERS
New York   London

THE FLORIDA KEYS
Dive Guide

Contents

• **Miami**

Key
Biscayne

N

FLORIDA

*Biscayne
National
Park*

*John Pennekamp
Coral Reef State
Park*

▼ **1, 2**
Carysfort Reef

▼ **3**
▼ **4, 5, 6, 7**
▼ **8**

*Everglades
National Park*

Key Largo ●

KEY LARGO

*Key Largo National
Marine Sanctuary*

Rock Harbor ●

CAPE SABLE

▼ **9**
▼ **10, 11**
▼ **12, 13**

*Gulf
of
Mexico*

Florida Bay

PLANTATION KEY

14, 15
▼ **16**
▼ **17**

Islamorada ●

*Great White Heron
National Wildlife
Refuge*

LONG KEY

Alligator Reef

Marathon ●

BOOT KEY

▼
18, 19

▼ **20**

Sombrero Key

Atlantic Ocean

INTRODUCTION

I made my first dive in the Florida Keys in 1971, on Elbow Reef. I still remember the dive vividly—there was so much life and the bright sun made the colors so intense. Memorable images filled the dive. On top of a ridge I saw a green moray eel slither by a closely packed school of iridescent blue-and-yellow grunts beneath a towering tree of golden brown elkhorn coral. In the clear blue water overhead a dozen silver barracuda hovered, motionless, perfectly lined up and reminiscent of arrows in a target.

From 1984 to 1987 I managed the Key Largo National Marine Sanctuary.

I became very familiar with the reefs in the Upper Keys and learned to revere the diversity of their underwater life. Every day held the promise of learning something new about the ocean. I discovered that there are few ecological communities on earth with the beauty, resilience, and fragility of these coral reefs.

I have made hundreds of dives here since then, and the reefs have had a special gift for me each time. Schools of surgeonfish, picking at the algae on the base of the elkhorn branches, enveloped me on Carysfort Reef. Green sea turtles looked right into my mask on Sombrero Reef. A helmet conch crawled slowly over my hand on the sand at Key Largo Dry Rocks. A great hammerhead shark gave me goose bumps at Looe Key. Four silver tarpon swam circles around me at Pickles Reef. A family of spotted eagle rays glided by me on Molasses Reef. Once a pod of 5 bottlenose dolphins swam right up to me in 4 feet (1.2 meters) of water in Florida Bay. Not every dive has offered such dramatic images, but they have all been a delight.

The Florida Keys are waiting to give their gifts to you, too. Come and see the magic of life beneath the water here. Take some time before you come to learn about the corals, fish, and marine invertebrates you will see. Spend some time poking around the sea grass and patch reefs, and paddle a canoe through the mangroves. Find out how all these creatures rely on each other. You will go home with the gift of memories you couldn't get anywhere else. You can return the gift by diving the reefs with care—you will earn the respect of everyone who loves the Florida Keys.

WILLIAM HARRIGAN

I began my scuba diving career in California while a graduate student in 1971. One of my classmates told me about a place he had been the previous summer. The waters offered over 100 feet (30.4 meters) of visibility, were warm enough to dive in without a wet suit, and provided home to countless schools of colorful tropical fish. Since all I had seen of the ocean so far was cold, not particularly colorful, and dominated by kelp rather than coral reef, I put it all down to hyperbole. His fantasy reef was in the Florida Keys. Little did I know what this string of islands would one day mean to me.

A

B

A. A friendly gray angelfish, Pomacanthus arcuatus, *swims on Molasses Reef.*

B. A barracuda, Sphyraena barracuda, *over the wreck of the* Cayman Salvage Master.

C. A diver examines deepwater corals growing on the crow's nest of the Bibb.

By 1978 I had done some diving in tropical waters, so I now believed that warm, clear water was possible. Until I finally visited the Florida Keys in the summer of that year I never imagined fish could school in such prodigious numbers or that they could be so friendly. The diving here made such an impression on me that by November I had quit my job in a custom color printing laboratory in Colorado and had moved to Key Largo to open an underwater photography center.

During those early years I had few customers and little to do but go diving. Most afternoons I went out with my friends who ran local dive boats. It was on reefs such as Molasses, French, Pickles, and the Elbow that I truly learned underwater photography. I shot fish portraits on the local reefs, practicing my macrophotography and close-up techniques. The next day I processed the film and learned by trial and error what worked and what did not. After I had been in business for a year or so, a dive magazine asked me to do an article on the reefs of the Middle Keys. Of course, I said yes even though I had yet to shoot a roll of wide-angle film underwater. With a borrowed lens and plenty of naïveté I went to Marathon to shoot my first editorial assignment in 1980. Thanks more to the opportunities there than to my own skill, I got some good photographs. The magazine gratefully called back with more assignments, and I became an underwater photojournalist.

I have dived all over the world in the years since, but I still find great pleasure in diving the reefs of my home, the Florida Keys. When the seas are calm and warm, and the visibility is at its best, this can be absolutely world-class diving. The schools of fish are still immense, and the individual reef dwellers still tolerate the close approach necessary for high-quality underwater photography. Despite some ecological pressures on the reefs, certain elements of the Florida Keys dive portfolio have even improved, particularly the artificial reefs.

The dive operators of the Florida Keys have been very creative in deliberately sinking ships as artificial reefs and dive attractions. These are huge projects; hundreds of thousands of dollars

are needed to secure the necessary government permits and to buy a ship, clean it of potential contaminants, tow it to the Keys, and finally sink it.

I was involved in the *Bibb* and the *Duane* project, which was successfully completed in 1987. I felt that my small participation in this shipwreck project was a way to repay some measure of the debt I owe the underwater world of the Florida Keys. These wrecks offer new wonders for divers to enjoy and, perhaps more importantly, offer a new environment for coral, sponge, and fish to colonize.

My wife and I have a daughter who is now 5 years old. Last summer our

family goal was to teach her to snorkel, not just in a swimming pool but out on the coral reef. Her first snorkel experience was at the Christ of the Abyss statue, and it gave her a great thrill to be in the place that she had seen so often in magazines and on my photographer's light table. She was amazed at the tropical fish and the splendor of our Florida Keys reef. I hope she will be able to share the same experience with her own children some day.

STEPHEN FRINK

History of the Florida Keys

The story of the Florida Keys has 2 parts of particular interest to divers. First, its geology, which tells how the reefs formed and why this reef system is such a popular dive destination today. Second, its history of human endeavor—a story of exploration, adventure, and perseverance that the people of the Florida Keys today still reflect. We start with the geologic origins, settled long before man arrived.

GEOLOGIC HISTORY

The rise and fall of the oceans as the great ice fields advanced and retreated ultimately resulted in present-day coral reefs and islands. The geologic foundation for these islands was laid as the earth cooled during the Pleistocene epoch many thousands of years ago. The polar caps expanded, lowering sea levels worldwide, gradually making conditions favorable for coral reef development off the south coast of Florida. A warm period followed (about 150,000 years ago), known as the Sangamon Interglacial, which raised sea levels 25 feet (7.6 meters) higher than they are today. All of what is now the Florida Keys was under water. This created a giant living coral reef that stretched from Miami to the Dry Tortugas.

The bedrock of the Upper Keys is made up of the limestone secreted by those ancient corals. The foundations of the Lower Keys reefs and islands, called oolitic rock, formed from the limestone remains of calcareous algae from these reefs. The fossil remains of these reefs are everywhere in the Florida Keys today, lying beneath the thin layer of topsoil.

Sea levels continued to rise and fall, leaving evidence of various distinct bands of coral reef. During the Holocene epoch more global warming occurred. About 5,000 years ago Florida Bay formed when water from melting ice caps spread over the low-lying land mass to mingle with the Gulf of Mexico and Atlantic Ocean. The Everglades also emerged, and what was once a contiguous peninsula became more than 200 islands that now comprise the Florida Keys.

If you examine a nautical chart of the Florida Keys, you will see that the islands form an arc, stretching from the southern end of the Florida peninsula, first to the south and gradually turning to the west. On the Atlantic side of the Keys there is a deep trough that curves with the islands. This is Hawk Channel, an ancient riverbed from a time when the water level was much lower. Hawk Channel is 15 to 20 feet (4.6 to 6 meters) deep, with a mostly silt bottom that does not support much coral growth but is valuable for boat navigation. Seaward of Hawk Channel the water gets shallow again and the bottom becomes sandy with exposed fossil coral. This hard bottom is the foundation for the reefs we dive today. The ridges that are now covered with living coral are the result of 5,000 or 6,000 years of accumulated calcium carbonate deposits by coral polyps.

A

A. This photograph from the 1991 space shuttle shows southern Florida covered by clouds. The Keys remain relatively clear—even the blue depths and the reefs can be seen.

EXPLORATION AND SETTLEMENT OF THE FLORIDA KEYS

The earliest residents were probably the Vescayos and Matecumbes Indians, followed later by the Caloosas. The first Indians were nomadic tribes who traversed the Florida Keys in carved boats, called pirogues, living on fish, turtles, manatees, and shellfish. Middens found in the Florida Keys, consisting of mounds of fish bones and conch shells left over from food eaten by these early explorers, date to 800 A.D.

Modern exploration began when the Spaniards sighted the Florida Keys in the early 1500s. Ponce de Leon sailed past in 1513, perhaps searching for the mythical Fountain of Youth. The twisted and misshapen form of the islands viewed from the sea inspired the men on this expedition to call them "Los Martires," the martyrs. There was scant fresh water, no gold, and too little topsoil to invite agricultural interest by the Spanish. The only explorations they conducted on the islands were to establish bases for salvage operations when their ships ran aground on the coral reefs. Consequently, unlike the islands of the Caribbean that were established centers of commerce by the 1600s, the Florida Keys remained largely dormant during the 250 years they were owned by Spain.

Some of Spain's most important contributions to the history of the Florida Keys occurred as a result of the weather or, more precisely, the severe weather produced by hurricanes. The Spanish galleon *Atocha*, loaded with gold, silver, and precious jewels, was hit by a hurricane and sunk in the Florida Keys in 1622. After years of searching and considerable financial and personal expense, treasure hunter Mel Fisher finally discovered the *Atocha* in 1985. Many of the artifacts recovered from the wreck are now on display in Key West. They tell a fascinating story of the Florida Keys maritime history, the science of treasure hunting, and the fabulous wealth that accompanies the right discovery.

In 1733 a fleet of 21 Spanish galleons, loaded with more loot from

B. This image shows a collection of artifacts from various Florida Keys shipwrecks.

C. These silver bars were found in the Atocha, *a Spanish galleon sunk off the Marquesas Keys in 1622 and found by Mel Fisher in 1985.*

B

C

the New World, left Havana for Spain. However, there was no National Hurricane Center in those days to advise sailors of impending foul weather. They set off under clear sky and fair winds but by the time they reached the Upper Keys a fierce hurricane sank all but one of the vessels. In the 1950s treasure hunter Art McKee had the first success in finding the remains of the ships and their treasure. This former hard-hat diver

spawned an active treasure industry in the Upper Keys, which flourished in the 1960s. Increased government regulation and decreased yields from the various wreck sites resulted in the decline of the treasure salvage industry by the mid-1970s. Many of the artifacts and even some of the booty from these local wrecks are in museums and treasure shops on Plantation Key and Key Largo.

Bahamians accounted for much

of the settlement of the Keys during the 1700s, coming over from those islands to cut wood and catch turtles. They brought their traditions to their new home, including their dietary dependence on a tasty gastropod known as the queen conch, *Strombus gigas.* As a result, a long-time resident of the Florida Keys is now known locally as a "conch."

The first true settlement in the Keys was at *Cayo Hueso,* Key West, in the early 1820s. This is the only deepwater port in these islands, even better than Miami, which has the drawback of the shallow waters (12 feet [3.6 meters]) of Biscayne Bay. Key West quickly became the headquarters for the wreckers, a wild group of men who sailed out to salvage ships and their cargoes once

innovative "screw-pile" design allowed construction of an open-framed structure on the reef, and many of these lighthouses continue to operate today. The lights on Sand Key, Sombrero Reef, Alligator Reef, and Carysfort Reef are all examples of screw-pile design lighthouses from this era.

Other industries briefly flourished in the Florida Keys, including hunting for sponges (sponging) and turtles and, perhaps, even piracy. The more enduring inhabitants were the families who lived throughout the Florida Keys in the 1800s, homesteading on the Atlantic side of the islands. They supported themselves by fishing and by planting melons, coconuts, and pineapples. Inter-island transportation was by shallow-draft boat, and any

they ran aground on the Florida Keys reefs. Although federal courts were established to keep the work of the wreckers orderly, there were many stories of false lights to lure unwary ships onto the reefs. The wreckers prospered for several decades, but the trade became less profitable when light ships were stationed at key points to mark the reefs. In the 1850s the light ships were replaced with ingenious lighthouses built on strategic reefs between Miami and Key West. Their

export of produce was by ferry to the port of Key West, where it was loaded onto schooners bound for northern ports.

All this changed in 1905 when Henry Flagler, president of the Florida East Coast Railroad, decided to lay track all the way from Homestead across the Everglades and along 30 of the islands of the Florida Keys to Key West. Known also as "Flagler's Folly" and "The Railroad That Went to Sea," Flagler's railroad forever changed the

nature of the Florida Keys, for better or worse.

The Overseas Railroad took 7 years and $27,000,000 to construct, an incredible cost in those days. Flagler's engineers and work crews were plagued by the heat, lack of fresh water, and mosquitoes. The inhospitable geography required expensive bridges and embankments to raise the rails above the sea. They finally prevailed but, although the railroad operated for 23 years, it never turned a profit.

A. The history of the Florida Keys is characterized by legends of wrecks, pirates, and treasure. This lithograph shows the infamous Blackbeard attacking an English vessel.

B. This ancient map depicts strange and fantastic creatures of the Atlantic Ocean, the Florida Peninsula, and the Keys.

Disaster struck on September 2, 1935, when a massive hurricane wiped out the railroad and killed 800 people. The 18-foot (5.5-meter) tidal wave and 200-mile-an-hour (322-kilometer-an-hour) winds of that hurricane not only destroyed the Key West Extension of the Florida East Coast Railroad, but also wiped out any thought of rebuilding it.

Flagler died soon after the railroad was complete, and no one remained with the motivation to resurrect his dream, even though most of the bridges had survived the hurricane intact. The railroad went into receivership, and the government bought the right-of-way and bridges for just $640,000. By this time the automobile was emerging as the popular choice for personal transportation and the Overseas Railroad became the Overseas Highway, with concrete replacing the rails all the way to Key West.

If Flagler had not built his railroad, would the Seven Mile Bridge or any of the other bridges exist today? Would the ferry boats that still carry automobiles between islands and regional airports become ever more crucial? Whatever might have been, the reality is that Flagler's Folly created the world's most accessible tropical paradise and made the Florida Keys "The Islands You Can Drive To."

Transportation

There are few dive destinations in the world as accessible to the traveler as the Florida Keys. Miami International Airport has convenient connections on all major airlines from nearly anywhere in the world. Frequent air service is available from Miami to both Marathon and Key West. Many visitors opt to rent a car and drive to the Keys, however. The drive from Miami International Airport to Key Largo is only slightly over an hour. The Overseas Highway runs 107 miles (172 kilometers) from Key Largo to Key West. It skips across the islands on a series of long bridges, including the famous Seven Mile Bridge, which stretches from Knight Key near Marathon to Little Duck Key. The drive is easy and scenic, with splendid views of Florida Bay and the Atlantic Ocean for most of the route.

A system of mile markers makes navigation simple. It begins with zero in Key West and counts up as you go toward Key Largo. Mile marker 107 is located just before you cross Jewfish Creek Bridge on the way out of the Florida Keys. Places in the Florida Keys are usually described by their mile marker and side of the road. For instance, the entrance to John Pennekamp Coral Reef State Park is at mile marker 102.9, oceanside. These mile markers are on both sides of the highway—small green rectangles with reflective numbers. When you see the numbers increase, you are headed north toward Key Largo; when you see them decrease, you are headed south toward Key West. The major population centers cluster around the following mile markers (MM):

Key West—MM0 through MM18
The Lower Keys—MM19 through MM45
The Middle Keys—MM46 through MM60
The Upper Keys—MM61 through MM107

There are hotels, motels, and camping areas all along this highway. Accommodations cover the complete range, from basic and economical to luxurious and expensive. Likewise, there are many restaurants to choose from, often with gorgeous water views. Everything from fast-food chains to uniquely traditional "Keys" restaurants can be found at frequent intervals. Visitors wishing to prepare their own meals will find numerous well-stocked supermarkets.

A

B

A. Aerial view of Marathon, looking south toward the Seven Mile Bridge, with boats in Boot Key Harbor.

B. View of the Overseas Highway looking southward across Upper Matecumbe and Lower Matecumbe, with the Channel Five Bridge in the distant background. This view shows the many channels between the islands and the extensive filling that was originally done in construction of Flagler's railroad (now the roadbed).

Climate

The Florida Keys are technically situated in the temperate zone. The Tropic of Cancer, the line of latitude that defines all things "tropical," is actually 70 miles (113 kilometers) south of Key West. However, the Florida Keys are significantly affected by the northward flow of the Gulf Stream, a huge ocean current that brings warm water from the Caribbean. The Gulf Stream brings warmer weather than would normally be expected. Winter temperatures in the Florida Keys usually reach a high during the day of about 75°F (24°C), with lows at night

about 72° (22°C). We who live here in the Florida Keys find the winter water temperatures dictate at least a 5-mm wet suit, but our visitors from more northern climates dive in T-shirts and bathing suits. Since most dives are 2-tank expeditions, even the hardiest diver can get chilled by the second dive. Wearing a wet suit in the winter is prudent.

The dress standards in the Florida Keys are very relaxed. Shorts, T-shirts, and sneakers or sandals are adequate in almost every circumstance. On formal occasions and in formal surroundings, dressier resort clothing may be appropriate. You will probably need a sweater or jacket when the temperature cools

around 65°F (18°C). High temperatures in the summer are usually near 90°F (32°C), with occasional higher peak temperatures. The sun shines strongly year round in the Florida Keys, making sunscreen a prudent precaution. Even when the sky is overcast the sun's ultraviolet radiation is still high, so use sun protection every day. Use at least a 15 SPF lotion to avoiding burning.

Water temperature also varies during the year. On the outer reefs, summer temperatures are generally a balmy 85°F (29°C). For these warm temperatures thermal protection is unnecessary, but a Lycra skin suit is advisable for protection from the sun and stinging sea creatures. In the winter it drops to

on winter evenings. In the winter a sweatshirt or warm-up suit sometimes helps prevent chilling during the boat ride back from the reef.

The weather in the Florida Keys is superb—warm temperatures, balmy breezes, and blue skies. However, visiting divers should be aware of several distinct weather patterns throughout the year. Summer tends, of course, to be warmer and, more important for divers, less windy. The usual northeast trade winds die down and the water gets flat and clear. There are more calm days from May to October than from November to April, and calm winds mean more comfortable boating and diving.

C. Traditional sailing ship on tour in Key West Harbor. Several similar vessels offer daily and sunset cruises.

D. The clear water and abundant coral of Looe Key is evident in this photograph of a boat on one of the mooring buoys. In the Keys divers can have

good visibility almost all year long—storms sometimes cloud the water from June to November.

E. Sunset, Key Largo, bayside. The tranquil waters of the bay provide spectacular views of the sunset from many locations in the Keys.

Tropical storms, including hurricanes, are the exceptions to this rule. The official tropical storm and hurricane season is from the beginning of June to the end of November, and the highest probability of storms is during the months of September and October. Residents take these storms seriously, particularly after viewing the devastation brought to the Homestead area by Hurricane Andrew in 1993. Fortunately, hurricanes can now be predicted with reasonable accuracy, allowing for a probable "hit-zone" and adequate time to evacuate. Therefore, hurricane season rarely affects tourism, and savvy divers come in masses to enjoy the good diving conditions typical in the summer and fall.

During the winter the trade winds are steadier, which causes the seas to be higher on average compared to the summer. The diving can still be excellent, but the ride is likely to be a bit bumpier. The other consideration brought by windy weather is decreased water clarity. These reefs are typically shallow with a sandy bottom, so big waves stir the bottom sand into suspension and degrade visibility. Fortunately, when the winds die down a single tidal shift can bring clear water back to the reef. Although the trade winds may blow more in winter, this part of the year tends to have fewer storms and less rain.

Visitors sometimes think the Florida Keys have only 2 seasons, winter and summer, or, perhaps, the wet season and the dry season. The change of seasons may be more subtle than in other latitudes, but there are definite differences. Even if spring and fall seem to last only a short time, they are excellent seasons for diving, with moderate temperatures and winds. Travelers at this time of year also enjoy lower prices in the hotels and more room on the dive boats. Actually, September and October often feature the best weather for diving and the least tourism.

A

B

C

A. In winter divers should use a 5mm wet suit, because the water temperature drops to 72°F (22°C).

B. Even if the temperature is quite warm in summer, about 85°F (29°C), divers should wear a Lycra skin to protect themselves from the sun and stinging creatures.

C. A diver, well protected in his wet suit, encounters a school of smallmouth grunts, Haemulon chrysargyreum, on the shallow coral fingers of Conch Reef.

D. This image is typical of the underwater paradise of the Keys. A blue angelfish, Holacanthus bermudensis, searches for food on the side of a coral-covered ridge.

Coral Reef Ecology

The reefs of the Florida Keys comprise the most northern barrier reef in the world and the only living coral reef in the continental United States. Over 40 species of coral and more than 500 species of reef fish are found on these reefs. At the heart of this complex and wonderful ecological world is the tiny coral polyp. The largest of these colonial animals is about the size of the tip of your little finger; most are much smaller. In spite of their small size, coral polyps build miles of intricate yet massive reefs.

E

D

F

numbers on the reef but are not reef builders themselves. They lack the symbiotic zooxanthellae and instead form flexible skeletons on the hard calcium carbonate skeletons of the boulder and branching corals. The tentacles of soft corals are usually extended to feed during the day as well as at night.

Many of the coral formations that live here now were alive when Catherine the Great ruled Russia and the American Revolution was still only a whisper of hope in the colonies to the north. The most frequently visited reefs have become dive icons known worldwide. Names such as Molasses Reef and Looe Key inspire divers to make the journey here to see for themselves the clear

Much of the reef-building ability of hard corals is due to their unique symbiotic relationship with tiny algae, called zooxanthellae. The zooxanthellae are responsible for the golden brown, yellow, or green colors of many corals, and contribute significantly to the energy production of the polyps. In the process of photosynthesis the zooxanthellae use the carbon dioxide and nitrogen waste of the polyp and produce oxygen and nutrients used, in turn, by the polyp. This photosynthesis requires sunlight, one of the reasons corals only grow in clear and reasonably shallow water. When the zooxanthellae remove the carbon dioxide and nitrogen, they also act as catalysts in the secretion of cal-

cium carbonate by the polyp. It is this calcium carbonate that forms the "skeleton" of the reef.

Coral polyps obtain the remainder of their nutrients by trapping plankton from the water with their tentacles, which contain stinging cells, called nematocysts. The tentacles of hard corals are normally withdrawn during the day when plankton is scarce. During this time, the polyps rely on the zooxanthellae to produce food. At night, when photosynthesis is not possible and plankton comes up from deeper water, the tentacles are extended and the polyps feed actively.

Soft corals, which generally have 8 tentacles, as opposed to the 6 tentacles found in hard corals, are found in great

water, massive coral heads, and abundant schools of fish. There is more to the Florida Keys than these famous reefs, however. This coral reef ecosystem is large and complex, with many interdependent parts. Visitors who see the stars but ignore the supporting cast are missing much of the story.

E. Soft corals are just one of the fascinating creatures that populate the Keys waters. They have a flexible skeleton and are generally referred to as "octocorals" because each polyp has 8 tentacles.

F. Colonies of elkhorn coral, Acropora palmata, *are quite common in the Keys. These specimens were photographed on Carysfort and South Carysfort Reefs.*

MANGROVE FORESTS

The reefs are linked to the land and to the surrounding shallows ecologically. Corals need clear, warm water to survive. They also needs water that does not contain too many nutrients; faster-growing organisms, such as algae, can compete successfully with corals for space. The plants on shore, particularly the mangroves, are essential in preserving the necessary water quality.

Mangroves are uniquely structured to living on the boundary between land and sea. Special adaptations allow them to tolerate salt water and long roots let them grow past the shore and into the water. The tangled miles of mangrove roots along the coast stabilize the land and prevent runoff from making the water turbid and overloaded with nutrients. They also provide protected habitat for many species of fish and invertebrates, particularly during the juvenile phase of the life cycle.

Snorkeling along the mangroves can be a fascinating experience. There is no telling what you might see. Hundreds of tiny fish hide among the roots, including snappers, mullet, wrasses, and even tiny barracuda. It is even possible to see manatees cruising through the mangrove channels, an especially good reason for boaters to be careful of their speed so that their propellers don't injure this gentle marine mammal. The under-

C

A

B

D

water portion of the mangrove root system is covered with sponges, anemones, and mollusks. For nonsnorkelers, a canoe or kayak is the perfect vehicle to see the mangroves up close—their silent propulsion does not startle the birds that make the mangroves their home, which consequently enhances photographic opportunities.

SEA GRASS

Unlike algae, sea grass actually has roots. It grows underwater, but is much the same as the grass on a lawn. (Fortunately, we don't have to spend our Sunday afternoons mowing it!) The Florida Keys reefs benefit from the presence of several species of sea grass, most notably turtle grass and eel grass. These 2 grasses often grow in the same area, but can be easily differentiated—turtle grass has flat blades and eel grass has round blades. Sea grasses are incredibly efficient in trapping particles in the water and binding up sediments. The root system can be as long as 3 feet (1 meter), with many wandering tendrils that weave the bottom into a thick mat. The blades of grass also trap many sediments, giving the grasses a typically fuzzy appearance. This helps keep the water clear for the corals on the reefs.

Like other green plants, sea grass uses photosynthesis for its energy needs and releases oxygen, which is also vital to the coral reef ecosystem. When you snorkel or dive near a sea grass bed, you can actually see oxygen released in the form of bubbles. Sea grasses also function as nurseries, providing homes for many of the juveniles of fish and invertebrates that later make their way out to the reef. Finally, sea grasses are an important food source. Herbivores of all types graze regularly on sea grass, including a variety of fish and turtles. Many of the fish that reside on the near shore reefs during the day leave the shelter of the reefs at night to feed on the surrounding sea grass. Their constant grazing creates a halo of clear sandy bottom around the reef that can be seen easily from above the reef.

A. The mangrove islands in Florida Bay are an important part of the coral reef ecosystem often overlooked by divers.

B. In this photograph taken during high tide the strong influence of the water on the mangrove ecosystem is evident.

C. This extraordinary aerial view shows the green mangrove area, the light blue shallow reefs, and the blue depths of the Keys.

D. With an underwater camera you can capture the rich life that populates the mangroves during high tide.

E. The mangroves are a fascinating and productive part of the coral reef ecosystem. One of the best ways of enjoying them is by kayak or canoe. Kayak and canoe rentals are available at many locations in the Keys.

F. Many divers are unaware of the importance of the sea grass beds, which stabilize the bottom and prevent harmful sedimentation. They also provide habitats and food for many creatures, including this juvenile grunt living in the turtle grass.

G. Sea grass beds also provide a habitat for this balloonfish, Diodon holocanthus, hiding in a bed of mixed manatee and turtle grass.

H. This longsnout seahorse, Hippocampus reidi, changes color to match the sponges growing amidst the manatee grass.

PATCH REEFS

Close to shore, corals may grow wherever a bit of hard substrate sticks up out of the sand or mud. The result is called a patch reef. These reefs are usually found in shallow water and grow vertically to the point where they sometimes break the surface at low tide. They often grow close to one another and in large numbers. Basin Hill Shoals off the north coast of Key Largo is an example of an extensive patch reef area. Patch reefs usually have a round shape, with hard corals in the center. Wherever there is room, a variety of soft corals also grow, sometimes visually dominating the reef.

A

B

C

D

A. Clear, deep water and plentiful reef fish make the Elbow's coral ridges a favorite location for divers.

B. Large colonies of elkhorn coral, Acropora palmata, *and staghorn coral,* Acropora cervicornis, *grow on the reefs of the Florida Keys.*

C. This aerial view of Sombrero Reef shows the coral formations that characterize most of the Keys area.

D. A diver swims with large schools of reef fish on Molasses Reef.

These reefs are often packed with juvenile reef fish, which spend the early part of their lives here before migrating to the deeper reefs. The complexity of life on a coral reef can be observed even on the smallest patch reef. Corals compete for space with each other and with other organisms, such as algae, sponges, and colonial anemones. Parrotfish feed on the coral polyps, and angelfish feed on the sponges. Schools of small fish shelter within the coral, and predators, such as jacks, swoop in to feed on them.

INNER BANK REEFS

Farther from shore than the patch reefs, but not as far out as the Outer Bank Reefs, there are reefs that have the characteristics of both. Key Largo Dry Rocks is a prime example of an inner bank reef. The shoreward side of the reef resembles a patch reef, while the seaward side is more like an outer bank reef. These differences mean that the reef is accessible to divers all the way around and there is good coral cover across the entire top of the reef. Inner bank reefs are also somewhat more protected when the weather kicks up and may offer good diving even when the outer bank reefs get uncomfortable due to waves and surge.

OUTER BANK REEFS

Often simply called bank reefs, these are the reefs with famous names that have attracted divers for decades. Reefs such as the Elbow, French, Molasses, Sombrero, and Looe Key have entertained literally millions of divers and will thrill millions more in the years to come. The dominant feature of the bank reef is a formation of coral ridges and sand channels, commonly called a "spur-and-groove" system. The ridges have been formed by the accumulated calcium carbonate secretions of thousands of years of coral growth. Corals living on top of these ridges contribute their own tiny amounts of calcium carbonate, or limestone, to the reef each day.

The ridges always run perpendicular to the shore, from shallow to deep water. Knowing how the ridges are

E. Penetrating sun rays show the structure of this elkhorn coral on one of the shallow coral spurs at Western Dry Rocks.

F. Close to the coral reefs divers can often observe large schools of shining fish. Here is a closely packed school of snappers and grunts.

G

E

H

F

G. Dives on the Elbow's coral ridges, as well as on other reefs, are characterized by clear water and plentiful reef fish.

H. In the open-water areas of the coral spurs on the center of Molasses Reef, divers can observe horse-eye jacks, Caranx latus, *schooling.*

oriented can make navigation simple. When swimming parallel to the shore, just count the ridges as you cross them. When swimming perpendicular to the shore, just keep track of whether you are going toward shallower or deeper water.

Bank reefs have a reef crest that is predominately coral rubble, deposited in the shallows by the force of wave action across the reef. Shoreward of the reef crest is a back reef area that is mostly sand and sea grass. When the spur-and-groove system reaches water about 30 to 35 feet (9 to 10.6 meters) deep, it starts to flatten. This is called the intermediate reef area, where soft corals and sponges begin to grow prolifically and coral boulders tend to be low and broad. As the reef slopes to 45 to 50 feet (13.7 to 15.2 meters), further changes are evident: sponges are larger and the coral ridges become even lower; species of sea fan, sponge, and gorgonian that grow best in deep water take the place of other corals. The deep reef includes the area from about 50 feet (15.2 meters) deep to the point where the reef levels out in the sand at depths between 70 and 100 feet (21.3 and 30.4 meters). This section is not well developed on all reefs, but Molasses Reef and Looe Key have extensive deep reef areas with small barrel sponges. Portions of the deep reef drop off steeply, forming mini-walls.

Although each of the habitats have been individually described, they are all essential, interrelated parts of the same ecosystem. None of them can be altered without affecting the others. As you dive the Florida Keys, learning about these different habitats will increase your appreciation for these fascinating reefs significantly.

Marine Parks and Sanctuaries

In the 1950s, when scuba diving was in its infancy, people were discovering the real treasure of the Florida Keys for the first time—not gold or the fountain of youth, but one of the most extensive coral reefs in the world. Unfortunately, as word of the beautiful corals spread, a new breed of reef wrecker arrived. Corals were pried and removed with dynamite from the reef to be sold in curio stands on the Overseas Highway; the tropical fish were collected or speared indiscriminately.

PENNEKAMP PARK

By 1957 there was a growing realization that these precious reefs needed protection. In an effort spearheaded by scientists such as Gilbert Voss of the University of Miami and conservationists such as John Pennekamp of the Miami Herald, the reefs were finally declared a state park in December of 1960. John Pennekamp Coral Reef State Park originally extended 20 nautical miles (37 kilometers) from Angelfish Creek in the north to Rodriguez Key in the south; the east-west boundary went out from the shore about 6 miles (9.6 kilometers) to the point outside the reefs at which the water depth reaches 60 feet (18.2 meters).

KEY LARGO NATIONAL MARINE SANCTUARY

A ruling by the Supreme Court in 1974 on a case relating to Florida's authority offshore established that the state only had jurisdiction over 3 nautical miles (5.5 kilometers). The result of this ruling was that the eastern boundary of Pennekamp Park was moved inshore, leaving most of the popular reefs unprotected. This potentially perilous situation did not last long: the Key Largo National Marine Sanctuary, managed by the National Oceanic and Atmospheric Administration (NOAA), was quickly designated and established a new umbrella of federal protection for the reefs.

The eastern boundary of the new

A. In addition to Fort Jefferson, there are many excellent diving and snorkeling areas in the Dry Tortugas, accessible only by boat or seaplane.

B. Fort Jefferson National Monument in the Dry Tortugas is now protected by the National Park Service.

sanctuary was moved out to the 300-foot (91.4-meter) depth contour to provide an extra buffer for the reefs. Both Pennekamp Park and the Key Largo National Marine Sanctuary continue to exist side by side, although most divers are not aware of the shared administrative responsibilities of the 2 protected areas. The reefs are protected and that is all that matters.

With the help of local dive operators and the community, the park and sanctuary implemented projects such as public mooring buoys, reef reports, boat ramp information signs, videos, underwater photography contests, sanctuary and park patrols, research and monitoring, and special education programs that have significantly reduced the damage that was being caused to the reef by visitors each year.

LOOE KEY NATIONAL MARINE SANCTUARY

Meanwhile, in the Lower Keys, the community around Looe Key was also realizing that something needed to be

done to protect the resources of this spectacular bank reef. Spear fishing had decimated the fish population: predator fish, such as jacks and groupers, were no longer seen on the reef. Lobster had been harvested to extremely low population levels. In 1982 the Looe Key National Marine Sanctuary was designated. At 7 square miles (18 square kilometers) it was the smallest of the marine sanctuaries, but it was also one of the busiest. Programs similar to those at Key Largo were initiated with great success.

FORT JEFFERSON NATIONAL MONUMENT

The Florida Keys reefs were also aided by the existence of 3 national parks. At the western end of the Keys, beyond the end of the Overseas Highway, Fort Jefferson National Monument protects the reefs, islands, and historic fort in the Dry Tortugas. This park is accessible by boat or seaplane only. Many people make the journey not only to dive or snorkel, but to tour the fascinating structure of Fort Jefferson. This bastion was erected just prior to the Civil War, but never saw any action. It was later turned into a prison and housed the infamous Dr. Samuel Mudd, among others. Most visitors are limited to snorkeling, but passengers on private boats and live-aboard dive boats can enjoy the excellent scuba diving in the Dry Tortugas.

EVERGLADES NATIONAL PARK

Many divers never realize the benefits they enjoy from the existence of the Everglades National Park, which actually preceded the establishment of Pennekamp Park. This large park protects not only the Everglades, but also a significant portion of Florida Bay. Both of these areas are vital to the long-term health of the Florida Keys coral reefs, providing nursery areas for fish and invertebrates. The proper flow of water through the "River of Grass," as the Everglades have been called, is important for the health of the Florida Bay sea grass beds, which, in turn, are essential to the reefs.

Although visitors to the Keys will probably not visit the Everglades National Park with any of the local dive operators, many excellent snorkeling spots in the park can be reached by small boat from the Keys. A land visit to the park is a great choice for a morning or afternoon when diving is not planned. Alligators are commonly found along popular spots, such as the Anhinga Trail, and bird-watching enthusiasts travel from all over the world to view the concentrations of tropical wading birds.

BISCAYNE NATIONAL PARK

The Overseas Highway cuts through the Everglades and turns south when it reaches Key Largo. However, there are more islands and coral reefs to the north of Key Largo, as well as a large bay called Card Sound. Fortunately, these are protected by the Biscayne National Park. Because of the proximity of these reefs to the rest of the Florida Keys, this national park is important

D

E

C. The Florida Everglades are considered the natural nursery to many juvenile reef fish.

D. This aerial view shows part of the Florida Everglades, also known in the Keys as the "Back Country."

E. Manatees are often found in the canals and along the shoreline of the Florida Keys, seeking warmer waters for the winter.

C

in ensuring good water quality and healthy reefs. Diving in Biscayne National Park is done by private boat or with a diving concession located within the park itself. A series of patch reefs, bank reefs, and a number of historical and modern shipwrecks provide ample dive incentive here.

NATIONAL WILDLIFE REFUGES

Three areas in the Florida Keys have been designated as National Wildlife Refuges by agreement between the United States Fish and Wildlife Service and the State of Florida. Situated in either Florida Bay or the Gulf of Mexico, these refuges include the Key West National Wildlife Refuge, the Great White Heron National Wildlife Refuge, and the Crocodile Lake National Wildlife Refuge. In addition to protecting the nesting grounds and feeding areas of sea birds and the endangered American crocodile, these areas are also important in the overall health of Florida Bay and, by extension, the coral reef.

FLORIDA KEYS NATIONAL MARINE SANCTUARY

In spite of the protection afforded by the parks and sanctuaries already established, by 1990 it was apparent that many areas of the Florida Keys reef system needed more attention. A series of serious ship groundings by large commercial vessels from 1987 to 1990 destroyed hundreds of square meters of living coral. Conflicts were occurring among commercial fishermen, sport fishermen, and divers, especially around the most popular reefs. Water quality in Florida Bay, in many of the residential canal systems, and even on the reef itself raised concerns about sewage disposal

dozens of county, state, and federal agencies, as well as many different private-interest groups, the management plan became law in 1997. The result is a compromise that is aimed at allowing activities, such as diving, that do not cause long-term damage, while restricting activities that may potentially harm the marine ecosystem.

Several new features of interest to divers have been incorporated into the Florida Keys National Marine Sanctuary (FKNMS). Eighteen areas of special protection called Sanctuary Preservation Areas (SPAs) have been established, mostly around the most heavily visited reefs. In the SPAs, mooring buoys have been provided and anchoring is discour-

and water flow. No matter how carefully we dive, people place a burden on the reefs each day by using toilets, throwing away trash, and operating engines.

In a bold move to jump-start the process of establishing protection for the entire Florida Keys coral reef ecosystem, the United States Congress passed the Florida Keys National Marine Sanctuary Act in 1990. This remarkable piece of legislation officially created the Sanctuary, but left it to NOAA, the State of Florida, and the Environmental Protection Agency to develop a management plan and determine the regulations. After an agonizingly long and contentious period of development that involved literally

aged. When a boat is anchored for diving, the anchor must not touch the coral and it must be checked by the first diver down before the dive proceeds. Touching, breaking, or disturbing any coral is prohibited. In most SPAs fishing by any means is not allowed. The SPAs are marked by round yellow buoys. Four areas have been set aside for research only; diving and fishing are not allowed. Research-only areas are located near Conch Reef, Looe Key, Eastern Sambo, and Tennessee Reef. If you dive with an established Florida Keys dive operator, you will not have to worry about straying accidentally into one of these research areas. If you operate your own boat or a rental boat, however, check

A. This baby crocodile blends into the habitat in the Crocodile Lake National Wildlife Refuge.

B. A great white heron graces the Florida Keys waters with its regal presence.

C. NOAA's Aquarius Undersea Habitat, operated by the National Undersea Research Center, is manned by scientists and support crews for extended coral reef research projects.

with the FKNMS for the exact boundaries of these areas.

Another zone that divers should be aware of is the Ecological Reserve. The rules in these areas are very similar to SPAs. One Ecological Reserve has been established in the vicinity of Western Sambo with a second to follow in several years near the Dry Tortugas.

When the Florida Keys National Marine Sanctuary was established, it was decided to keep Pennekamp Park and the 2 sanctuaries at Key Largo and Looe Key intact as well, even though they are technically included within the larger sanctuary. These areas still provide some important additional protection and are generally well known to people.

As far as divers are concerned, the regulations of the various parks and marine sanctuaries are about the same, although regulations are more strict in the SPAs and Ecological Reserves. A brief summary of these rules includes:

- Do not touch the coral.

- Do not anchor in the coral. Carefully place your anchor in the sand, ensuring that the anchor chain and line do not contact the coral.

- Do not litter. Plastic items (e.g., sandwich wrappers and bags) can be particularly harmful.

- Do not damage or remove historical artifacts or scientific equipment.

- Operate vessels at idle speed in the vicinity of stationary vessels, residential shorelines, shallow reefs, and displayed divers' flags.

- Do not run aground or operate a vessel in such shallow water that the prop scars the bottom.

- Spear fishing is prohibited in most areas of the Florida Keys. Check with the FKNMS for regulations and specific areas for spear fishing.

- Always display a diver's flag when diving or snorkeling.

This list of regulations is very important, but the sanctuary is more about

the list of things you are encouraged to do. Safe diving and snorkeling are at the top of this list, and the sanctuary has been established to ensure that divers are able to enjoy these beautiful reefs for many generations to come. For information about the natural resources or rules of the sanctuary contact one of the sanctuary offices in Key Largo, Marathon, or Key West. Any of the Keys Chambers of Commerce or dive operators can also provide information. By radio, call "Sanctuary Patrol" on Channel 16 for information or assistance.

D. *Blue angelfish,* Holacanthus bermu- densis, *are one of the most colorful fish species in the Keys waters.*

E. *This old loggerhead turtle,* Caretta caretta, *swims among the sea plumes between the reefs at Coffins Patch.*

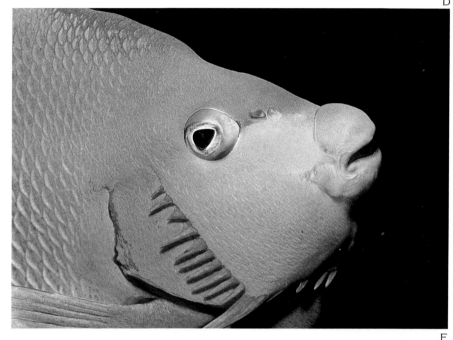

D

E

Diving in the Florida Keys

Divers coming to the Florida Keys should realize that there is no shore diving. The only interesting diving close to shore is along the mangrove forests, most of which are inaccessible from land. In any case, the mangroves are so shallow that they are more suitable for snorkeling than diving. All of the popular diving reefs are located 3 to 6 miles (4.8 to 9.6 kilometers) offshore. This geographic situation is one of the reasons that the Florida Keys reefs are in good health, however,

essential and should be used in conjunction with both a depth sounder and a Global Positioning System (GPS) receiver. The most important means of navigating, however, is the eye. Shallow coral reefs look darker than the surrounding water; you can usually see the green or brown color of the coral. Polarizing sunglasses significantly improve your ability to "read the water." Having the sun at your back and high in the sky is also important to navigating by eye. Even the local professionals will take the long way around when the lighting is not good for reading the bottom. Chart a careful course in deep water from navigation aid to navigation aid.

throughout the Florida Keys. The large number of high-quality dive operations in the Florida Keys makes diving here extremely convenient. Regular boat schedules allow divers to choose up to 5 dives a day; they can arrange their dive schedule to satisfy their own desires.

Dive boats in the Florida Keys, like commercial boats everywhere in the United States, are regulated by the United States Coast Guard. The strict standards set by the Coast Guard ensure that divers travel in seaworthy vessels with competent captains. Each operation must meet the Coast Guard specifications for construction, maintenance, safety equipment, and crew experience.

A

B

C

so the lack of shore diving actually benefits divers.

There are many convenient ways to get to the reefs. Private pleasure boats, rental boats, and commercial dive boats are all used by divers. If you are operating your own vessel, take the time to learn about navigating in the Florida Keys. There are few landmarks visible to guide the way and there are thousands of unmarked shallow reefs. This is definitely an area in which boating experience is crucial to avoid grounding your vessel and to find the best of the dive opportunities.

Visitors should be aware that fines for running aground on the reefs can be substantial. A large-scale chart is

Mooring buoys have been installed at all of the best dive sites to protect the coral from anchor damage. Brochures on their location and use are available at the marine parks and sanctuaries, as well as throughout the Florida Keys at marinas, hotels, and dive operations. These buoys are used on a first-come-first-served basis. Be sure to raise a divers' flag before you get in the water, so that other boaters will be warned to keep clear or slow down. When other boaters are waiting for buoys, it is courteous to vacate your buoy when you have stowed your gear after the dive.

By far the largest proportion of visiting divers use one of the many professional dive operations found

There are 2 basic types of commercial dive boat in service in the Florida Keys. The first is known locally as a "6-pack" because it is limited to carrying 6 passengers at a time. The Coast Guard inspection requirements are somewhat less stringent for 6-packs, but the boat and captain are still required to be licensed. Six-packs are popular among those seeking a more intimate, personalized dive experience. Some divers prefer the 6-pack operations because there are fewer divers aboard to potentially silt up the reef or interfere with underwater photographic opportunities. Most 6-pack boats range in size from 20 to 30 feet (6 to 9 meters), yet still have a dive platform with extended ladder, tank racks, and at least minimal marine electronics, such as a VHF radio and a GPS receiver. When conditions get rough, the 6-pack boats may be at a disadvantage compared to larger boats. A sea with 6-foot (1.8-meter) waves may still be manageable on a 50-foot (15.2-meter) boat, but can really toss a 30-foot (9-meter) vessel, making it very difficult to move about comfortably on the deck and reboard after the dive.

The second type of vessel is larger and has stricter Coast Guard inspection and equipment requirements than the 6-packs. Referred to as "multipassenger" boats, these larger dive boats typically range in size from 35 to 65 feet (10.6 to 19.8 meters). Some are mono-hulls and some are catamarans; most are powered by diesel engines. These vessels are stability tested and certified for as many as 48 scuba divers, yet they rarely run at full capacity. On a busy holiday weekend there can be a full complement of passengers, but there are usually only 8 to 20 divers. Because of their size, many of these boats have additional features—camera tables and gear storage facilities. Many have walk-through transoms to facilitate access to the stern and dive platforms with a pair of ladders rather than a single ladder.

Safety equipment (emergency oxygen and an extensive first-aid kit) is carried by 6-packs and multipassenger boats. Both types of vessel usually have fresh water on board, either a shower or a simple hose and nozzle. The captains and crews are all professional and most are very

D

E

F

A. The mangrove channels are like naturally occurring "creeks" that allow water to flow around and between the islands of the Keys.

B. Divers should snorkel through the mangroves to get a better understanding of their importance.

C. Mangrove snappers hide among mangrove roots on the bayside in Key Largo. The mangroves help keep the water clear on the reefs by stabilizing the land and preventing sedimentation. They also provide nursery grounds and food for fish.

D. This dive boat is typical of the well-equipped, professionally run commercial dive boats in the Keys.

E. Clear water, live coral, and lots of fish are the hallmarks of diving in the Keys.

F. Snorkelers prepare to enter the water in Key Largo. The hundreds of shallow reefs in the Keys are ideal for both snorkeling and diving.

experienced in delivering divers safely and comfortably to the best dive sites.

Most daily dive trips are 2-tank excursions, scheduled in the morning and in the afternoon. A trip to the reef takes at least half an hour in a fast boat and sometimes as long as 50 minutes in a slow boat, so it is usually impractical to run out and back for a single-tank dive. Many dive operators also schedule a single-tank night dive several times a week.

Weight belts and tanks may or may not be included in the price of the dive. Divers from outside the United States should be aware that dive boats in the Florida Keys provide tanks with U.S. standard valves. Regulators with DIN

yokes will not fit these tanks and most dive operators do not carry a DIN adapter. Divers with DIN equipment should bring a U.S. yoke for their regulator or a DIN adapter for U.S. tank valves, or plan on renting a regulator. Most operators carry a full line of rental equipment, so divers can arrive with only their certification cards and log books and still enjoy a comfortable dive.

Recreational dives are usually done in buddy teams, without a designated tour leader provided by the local dive operation. Unlike some destinations requiring all guests to follow a dive master, buddy teams are encouraged to dive the reefs at their own pace. Computer diving is allowed, provided both divers

A. This aerial view not only shows a typically equipped commercial dive boat but also gives evidence of the blue waters of the Keys.

B. A school of swift permit, Trachinotus falcatus, crosses the blue water over Molasses Reef.

C. The silver profile of a great barracuda, Sphyraena barracuda, in the clear blue waters.

D. The Eagle is a popular wreck dive. Here is the crow's nest on the aft mast about a year after the sinking in 1985.

in a buddy team have a computer. Sharing a single computer between 2 divers is not permitted.

Guided dives can be arranged easily, but requests for a dive guide should be made in advance at the dive shop. To make advanced dives without a guide, such as to deep wrecks, it may be necessary to show that dives under similar conditions have been logged recently. Naturally, all dive instruction is conducted under the guidance of a certified scuba instructor. At the dive site, the mate or dive master gives a briefing that describes the general conditions, underwater topography, and reef ecology.

Every dive operation has its own procedure, but divers are usually asked to ascertain the position of the boat at 1,000 psi (70 bar), and be back on board with 500 psi (35 bar) remaining in the tank. All dive operators in the Florida Keys require divers to have an alternate air source for safety. Bottom time is generally not limited artificially, but sometimes the diving is so shallow that the available bottom time is well over an hour. In these cases, in common courtesy to those who have consumed their air more quickly and are already back on the boat, a dive of an hour or less is the accepted norm. Divers are typically asked to ascend slowly and conduct a 3-minute safety stop at 15 feet (5 meters).

With the exception of 1 or 2 centers that offer specialty dives for the technical diver, all diving from charter dive boats is no-decompression. Recompression chambers are located in Miami, Marathon, and Plantation Key in case of an emergency. As in other dive destinations, diving accident insurance, such as that offered by DAN or PADI, is highly recommended.

Underwater visibility in the Florida Keys is generally excellent. However, it may vary considerably according to the weather, location, and time of day. The average visibility range is about 30 to 80 feet (9 to 24.3 meters). In the Upper Keys, visibility on the outer reefs depends more on the presence of blue water than on anything else. Blue water comes straight from the Gulf Stream, a kind of overflow from this great oceanic current. When the reefs have blue water, visibility can be 60 to 100 feet (18.2 to 30.4 meters), regardless of the weather. Tides are also not really important to divers because the long land mass of Key Largo, Plantation Key, and the other Upper Keys islands helps to keep the murky bayside water separate from the clear Atlantic water.

The Upper Keys inner reefs have their best visibility when the winds are calm. High winds stir up the bottom sediments, turning the water a milky green. When the weather is good, the inner reefs have 30 to 60 feet (9 to 18.2 meters) of visibility with green water. On rare occasions the blue water from the Gulf Stream also washes these inner reefs, making excellent conditions for both divers and snorkelers.

In the Lower Keys there are more large channels between the islands, so the state of the tide is a more important factor in the visibility equation. High winds still reduce the visibility on the inner reefs, but the outer reefs tend to have their lowest visibility on the outgoing tide. The outer reefs in the Lower Keys have best visibility when the blue water is in and the tide is right. Calm winds also tend to raise the visibility. As a result, visibility in the Lower Keys is somewhat more variable than in the Upper Keys. When the conditions are right, though, the Lower Keys can feature water clarity in the same 60-to-100-foot (18.2-to-30.4-meter) range.

Water temperature in the Florida Keys usually averages about 84°F (29°C) from June to September and about 72°F (23°C) from December to February. During the spring (March to May) the water temperature begins to rise between these highs and lows. From October to November it begins to descend. Divers are comfortable in summer wearing bathing suits, T-shirts, or Lycra suits. A neoprene wet suit is preferred in winter. Divers use anything from a shorty to a 7-mm wet suit. Polartec suits are a good option most of the year; however, divers who get cold easily will find them too thin in the winter.

E

F

G

E. A mixed school of grunts finds shelter next to one of the coral- and sponge-covered ridges at Molasses Reef.

G. This spotfin butterflyfish, Chaetodon ocellatus, *shows its nighttime colors.*

F. This rare blanket octopus, Tremoctopus violaceus, *was photographed on Molasses Reef.*

Coral Reef Diving Etiquette

S ome special considerations apply to diving in the Florida Keys, owing to the popularity of diving here and the fragile nature of coral reefs. Part common sense and part legal requirement, diving etiquette provides a set of guidelines for divers that is easy to follow and should not interfere in diving enjoyment. Following these simple rules ensures that you have the best dive possible and helps to preserve the reefs for others:

A

• Avoid all contact with living coral. No one visiting a palace would tramp through its splendid rose garden—a coral reef should receive the same respect. The touch of fins, tanks, or knees can crush the septa of coral polyps or remove the protective mucus coating. The damage caused by one diver is usually not visible, but the cumulative damage from hundreds of divers visiting the same reef year after year becomes obvious. Good buoyancy control keeps you clear of the coral as you swim along the reef.

• Do not wear gloves on reef dives when possible; this helps you avoid the temptation to touch unnecessarily.

B

C

Wreck diving, for which gloves may be required for safety and comfort, is the exception.

• Use sandy areas for contact with the bottom. When you must steady yourself or stop underwater, settle into one of the many sand patches. Sometimes you may need only to put a fin tip or hand down to control your motion. When this happens, look for sand. However, rise from the sand gently; the silt stirred up by a clumsy, overweighted diver can smother fragile coral polyps.

• Use the mooring buoys. The Florida Keys National Marine Sanctuary maintains a set of mooring buoys that are free for use and available on a

first-come-first-served basis. The moorings are located directly over nearly all of the favorite dive sites. If you rent a boat or arrive on your own, pick up a mooring buoy brochure before you go out to the reefs. The brochures can be found at dive shops, the Chamber of Commerce, the marine sanctuary office, and even at many hotels. The information in the brochure will help you select a dive site, find it on the water, and anchor safely.

• Do not feed the fish. Observing large schools of fish behaving naturally is one of the best features of diving in the Florida Keys. Although feeding is not specifically prohibited by the rules of the Florida Keys National Marine Sanctuary, it is strongly discouraged. Feeding the fish alters their behavior patterns and may be detrimental to their health. Enjoy the unique experience of drifting along with a school of horse-eye jacks or hundreds of yellow goatfish instead of creating a frenzied pack of scavengers.

• Spear fishing is not allowed in most of the waters of the Florida Keys. Check with the Florida Keys National Marine Sanctuary for areas in which you can use spear guns. Using or even possessing a spear gun in restricted areas results in confiscation of the gun and a stiff fine.

• Keep all trash aboard your boat. Plastics are a particular problem because they last so long and get wrapped around the coral. Most littering is inadvertent— a sandwich wrapper whipped off by the wind—so extra care is needed on the water.

• Respect the marine life. Harassing turtles or other sea life causes unnecessary and life-threatening stress. Enjoy your encounters with them, but do not attempt to ride them or touch them.

A. This diver is harassing puffers by making them blow themselves up. Do not do this.

B. Feeding the fish alters their natural behavior and is discouraged.

C. Standing on, touching, or disturbing the coral is not allowed in the Florida Keys.

HAZARDS TO AVOID

Diving in the Florida Keys is generally not strenuous or dangerous, but if you want to make sure your dive vacation is not unnecessarily interrupted by an injury there are a few potential hazards to avoid. Many divers may be surprised to find that sharks, barracuda, and moray eels are not at the top of the list. In fact, they are not even on the list because attacks by these animals are nearly nonexistent in the Florida Keys. At some dive sites, however, particularly on the Elbow Reef, barracuda and morays have been hand fed for many years. They are used to divers and may approach you closely. When this happens relax and enjoy the encounter. Waving your hands at a barracuda or eel is not a good idea—they may mistake your fingers for the bait fish they are often fed.

Here are some of the hazards that more often cause dive vacations to be cut short:

- *Sunburn.* Protection from the sun is essential in the Florida Keys. A tight wet suit definitely does not feel good on tender, sunburnt skin. Acclimatize your skin to the sun gradually, keep covered, and apply sunscreen. Sunburn strikes snorkelers frequently; it is easy to forget about the sun on your back when you are enjoying the water.
- *Sea lice.* This malady is actually caused by the microscopic larvae of thimble jellyfish. When the larvae get trapped next to your skin, especially along the edge of a bathing suit, they cause a slight swelling accompanied by itching and burning. Topical painkillers and antihistamine creams help to alleviate the problem, which goes away in a few days. Fortunately, sea lice are only a problem for a few months in the spring while the water warms up. Unfortunately, they are too small to see, so it is not simple to avoid them. They are most prevalent near the surface, so descending quickly on a dive sometimes helps.
- *Jellyfish.* There are several types of jellyfish in the Florida Keys that you can see and easily avoid. These include the Portuguese man-of-war, moon jellyfish, and the upside-down jellyfish. The

man-of-war floats on the surface, trailing long tentacles underwater, and causes by far the most severe stings of the local jellyfish species. Moon jellyfish have very short tentacles and round bodies up to a foot (30 centimeters) in diameter. Moon jellyfish are generally encountered from the surface down to about 20 feet (6 meters). Rarely will a moon jellyfish cause severe pain, but it can cause discomfort. Some people are more affected than others by jellyfish stings, just as some are more affected than others by bee stings on land. Upside-down jellyfish are more common in Florida Bay and in shallow water near the shore. They usually lie on the bottom, with the tentacles pointing upward. Any jellyfish sting can be treated with a paste of fresh water and meat tenderizer. For more severe stings or strong reactions, seek medical attention.

- *Coral cuts.* Divers are advised to avoid all contact with coral, so this should be a rare problem. However, some cuts are inevitable and should be treated properly. Coral cuts almost always become infected when they are not treated. As soon as possible, the affected area should be cleaned and a triple antibiotic ointment applied. Keep applying the ointment until the cut has healed completely.
- *Fire coral.* Contact with fire coral will not usually result in a cut, but you will definitely know that something is wrong. Touching this relative of the true corals results in a burning sensation that later begins to itch. The affected area also swells slightly. Pain-relief sprays and antihistamine lotions provide some relief, but the problem only lasts a day or two anyway. Extensive fire coral contact could be dangerous enough to merit seeking medical assistance. The best solution is to avoid contact with fire coral in the first place. There are 2 forms of fire coral, leafy fire coral and encrusting fire coral. Both are mustard brown in color with a white tinge near the edges. Fire coral can encrust anything underwater, from pilings and wrecks to other corals. If you are not sure what it looks like, get a dive master to point it out to you.
- *Stingrays.* A stingray has a barbed protrusion at the base of its tail that

D. The sea fans on the left side of this image are dead and have been covered with the dangerous branching fire coral, Millepora alcicornis. *The sea fan on the right is normal and healthy.*

E. Moon jellyfish, Aurelia aurita, *can sting bare skin, so divers should avoid them.*

D

E

can inject a particularly painful poison. Accidentally stepping on a stingray is about the only way to get stung, but underwater photographers have been known to get stung while trying to force a stingray into a particular pose. Treatment includes immersing the wounded area in warm water to help break down the toxin.

ANNUAL EVENTS

Diving is excellent all year long in the Florida Keys, but a number of events of special interest to divers occur annually. These events are entertaining and educational and can add to your diving enjoyment.

If you are in the Florida Keys during the months of August and September, plan on at least one night dive to view the annual coral spawning. Mass spawning is one of several means by which corals reproduce. Coral formations get larger, for instance, by the actual splitting of 1 polyp into 2. This method of reproduction is called budding. Coral colonies also spread by fragmenting, often caused by wave action breaking off a piece of coral and moving it to another location. Each year corals also reproduce sexually, releasing their larvae into the water in mass spawnings that are mysteriously synchronized with the passage of the full moon.

Although a great deal of research remains to be done before this event will be fully understood, its timing can be predicted with reasonable accuracy for several species of coral, including elkhorn and star corals. There may be several windows of time in which to view the spawning, each occurring about a week after the full moon. The event occurs at night, usually between the hours of 8 P.M. and 12 midnight. Information about the specific nights when spawning is anticipated to occur can be obtained from the FKNMS, and special trips to view the spawning are offered by a number of dive operators.

Sponges can release eggs and sperm or larvae into the water in similar mass spawnings. This event has also been observed in late summer, but details of the timing are even less predictable than for coral. When the brown tube sponges spawn they look like miniature volcanoes, spewing out long streams of larvae that are swept away in the current.

Another annual event that draws divers to the Florida Keys like metal filings to a magnet is the lobster mini-season. This 2-day event precedes the regular commercial lobster season, allowing divers to get a head start on the annual harvest of spiny lobsters. Bear in mind that there are actually 2 separate mini-seasons, 1 federal and 1 state; however, they are usually coordinated. The rules may vary each year and depend on whether you are in state or federal waters. In general, federal waters do not begin until you get 3 nautical miles

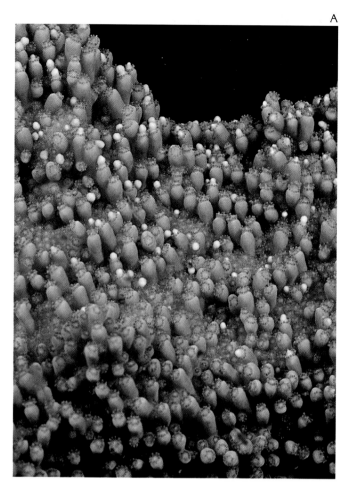

A. Spawning elkhorn coral on Key Largo Dry Rocks. This event occurs every year during August and September. About a week after the full moon during this period, corals release their larvae in a spectacular mass spawning event.

(5.5 kilometers) from shore. If you decide to take part in the mini-season, here are a few rules to follow:

- A license is required. This can be obtained at many locations for a nominal fee.
- All lobsters must be measured while in the water. Bringing a lobster back to the boat for measurement is not allowed. Lobsters must be taken whole and transported to shore whole. A net and tickle stick provide the best method to catch the lobster.
- Taking lobsters from traps is strictly forbidden.
- Egg-bearing lobsters of any size must be released unharmed.
- A limit is established each year; substantial fines can be incurred for exceeding the limit.
- Sanctuary Preservation Areas are out of bounds for lobster catching. Selected reef areas within Pennekamp Park may also be closed to lobstering.

The rules often change from year to year, so be sure to check with one of the park or sanctuary offices for up-to-date

information. During the mini-season, please do not let your zeal for catching lobsters result in damage to the coral.

The Reef Environmental Education Foundation (REEF), a nonprofit organization committed to protecting the marine environment, holds an annual fish survey that has been attracting a growing number of participants—an enjoyable and conservation-minded event. REEF's principal activity is the collection of fish distribution data in Florida, the Bahamas, the Caribbean, and the Gulf of Mexico for use in managing the reefs. Divers can take part in several week-long field surveys in the Florida Keys each year. Information can be obtained from REEF headquarters in Key Largo.

In July every year the reefs at Looe Key rock to the sounds of the Underwater Music Festival. During this unique one-day event participating dive boats hang waterproof speakers into the water and U.S. One Radio broadcasts a special selection of music on 104.7 FM. You can dive to the sounds of island music, reggae, rock, and jazz from 10 A.M. to 4 P.M. Dancing shoes, or rather fins, are not required. The Underwater Music Festival is scheduled for the first Saturday following the Fourth of July.

Underwater photographers of any experience level can enjoy the annual Key Largo Nikonos Shootout. This fun-filled event is usually scheduled in August or September, and attracts more divers than any other similar contest anywhere in the world. The format of the event puts everyone on equal footing. One day of shooting is devoted each to wide-angle, normal, and macro/close-up photography. Participants are issued a numbered roll of film each day, which must be turned in later the same day. The film is developed overnight and photographers examine their results and pick the photograph they wish to enter in that category. A panel of well-known professional photographers selects the winners, and prizes are awarded at the end of the contest. You may select your own dive site in the Key Largo area, but everyone dives the same day to shoot for the same category. There are also seminars, slide shows, cookouts, and parties, making this a week of pure diving fun and, of course, wonderful prizes courtesy of Nikon, various dive manufacturers, and local merchants.

B, C. Spawning brown tube sponges on Molasses Reef. Less is known about this event than the annual coral spawning, but it occurs in late summer and affects many sponges, which coat the reef with eggs and sperm.

D. Spiny lobsters, Panulirus argus, have been protected at Looe Key for more than a decade. The migration of these extraordinary crustaceans is famous in the Keys.

Underwater Photography

Some of the most stunning underwater photographs published each year are taken in the Florida Keys. Underwater photographers find the dive sites convenient and productive and have many reasons to love the location. On the shallow reefs, you will not run out of bottom time before you run out of film; many different species of fish are found in large schools, providing opportunities not found anywhere else; the clear, shallow water allows for the use of strong ambient light; there is an enormous variety of marine habitats; high-quality rental cameras and accessories are readily available at the many dive shops; the dive boats provide camera tables, rinse barrels, and assistance in handling gear; same-day E-6 slide processing and other underwater photographic services are available in Key Largo (at Stephen Frink Photographic, mile marker 102.9); the numerous shipwrecks provide superb photographic backgrounds; and even the fish are accustomed to the presence of divers and tolerate being approached closely. There are so many photographic possibilities on each reef, it is difficult to decide whether to set up for wide-angle, normal, or macrophotography.

WIDE-ANGLE PHOTOGRAPHY

A wide-angle lens is a good choice for the middle of the day when there is plenty of ambient light to brighten the background. From about 10 A.M. to 3 P.M. the sun is high in the sky and more of the sun's rays penetrate the water than at other times of the day. You can more easily balance the background available light exposure with the foreground strobe exposure. This is especially true for wide-angle photography on the deeper wrecks. Good sunlight gives you the intense blue background that really emphasizes the subject of the photograph. This is also a good time of day for using a wide-angle lens for available-light-only photographs in the

A. The photographer is studying a superb shot: a mixed school of schoolmasters and Caesar grunts beneath elkhorn coral at French Reef.

B. The Key Largo Nikonos Shootout, part of the popular Nikon "shootout" underwater photography contest series, held each fall in the Florida Keys.

shallow waters. Carysfort Reef, Key Largo Dry Rocks, North Dry Rocks, Coffins Patch, Looe Key, and Western Dry Rocks are excellent sites for these types of images.

If you happen to be in the Keys and the weather is not cooperating, wide-angle photography can still be a good choice, as long as you work close to the subject. Get in as tight as the lens allows and you will still bring back some superb wide-angle shots.

NORMAL PHOTOGRAPHY

The approachable fish life in the Florida Keys provides many good opportunities for lenses in the 28–60-mm range. All of the wrecks are good choices for fish photography. Reefs such as Molasses, Pickles, Davis, Coffins Patch, and Looe Key are known for the congregations of fish under ledges and schools of fish near the coral. For best results, shoot from about 3 feet (1 meter)—even closer when your lens and the fish behavior allows. Move in slowly and carefully to avoid spooking the fish

and you will capture those head-on, closely packed fish photographs that are so appealing.

In addition to the schools of fish there are many good single subjects that are the right size for normal-lens underwater photography. Sea turtles, nurse sharks, moray eels, and many coral formations are suitable subjects for normal lens photography. Do not expect to get good pictures of 6 of your dive buddies or the entire bow of the *Duane* shipwreck with a 35-mm lens. You would have to be too far away to get such subjects in your viewfinder, and the results are disappointing—rent a wide-angle lens so you can move in closer.

MACRO- AND CLOSE-UP PHOTOGRAPHY

You could jump in the water at any time and in any place in the Florida Keys with a macrophotography setup and come back with outstanding photographs. However, some of the most productive areas include the shallow reefs. Photographers have plenty of time here to search for just the right subject to fit in the limited confines of a macro framer. Reefs such as Horseshoe, Pickles, Delta Shoals, and Nine Foot Stake are packed with photogenic invertebrates and juvenile fish.

Night dives are another excellent time to mount a macro tube or close-up kit. Many colorful creatures come out at night all over the reefs and on the wrecks. In addition, it is easier to coax fish into a wire framer at night than during the day.

There are a few days in the Florida Keys when visibility is down and the sun is weak. When the weather is just not on your side, macrophotography is probably the way to go. Strobes provide

C

D

E

F

C. Wrecks are always considered excellent subjects for underwater photographers. Here is the upper deck of the Bibb.

D. The Christ of the Abyss statue, placed underwater at Key Largo Dry Rocks in 1966.

E. The Benwood is an excellent site for fish photography—hundreds of cooperative reef fish live here.

F. A diver encounters a friendly green moray eel, Gymnothorax funebris. It is quite hard to take good quality photographs while swimming.

all the light you need and the close camera-to-subject distance makes the water look gin clear again.

UNDERWATER PHOTOGRAPHY ETIQUETTE

There are a few things to keep in mind when photographing in the Florida Keys:

• Getting a good photograph is not a good excuse for damaging coral. A carefully placed fin tip or finger can let you steady yourself without contacting live coral—there are plenty of sand pockets on which you can stand. Photographers are expected to have excellent buoyancy control.

• Harassing the marine life for a photograph is also discouraged. Photographs of inflated pufferfish and of divers riding turtles only show lack of respect.

• Not everyone on a dive boat appreciates the value of photographic equipment. Make sure your camera is not placed where someone can carelessly damage it.

Here are a couple of etiquette tips for nonphotographers, too:

• When you come across a photographer underwater, don't swim in front of the camera, or allow your bubbles to rise into the photographer's view.

• Many photographers carry more than one camera or strobe, setting them carefully on the bottom when not in use. Expensive cameras are rarely dropped on the bottom and left there by accident, so look around for the photographer before you pick one up thinking you made the find of the century.

Carysfort Reef

GULF OF MEXICO

FLORIDA

Key Largo

Carysfort Reef

KEY LARGO

KEY LARGO NATIONAL
MARINE SANCTUARY

N

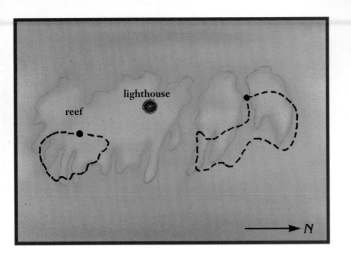

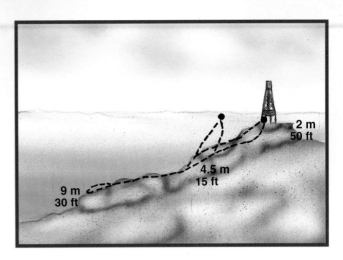

Although the spelling has changed over the years, Carysfort Reef is named for the British man-of-war *HMS Carysford*, which ran aground here on October 23, 1770. The shallow coral, which sticks up above water level during very low tides, claimed many other vessels over the years, including one of the light ships that was sent to mark it. To reduce the hazard that the reef posed to ships, a remarkable lighthouse was finally erected directly on top of the reef in 1852, using a recently invented "screw-pile" construction. The lighthouse was assembled in Philadelphia, Pennsylvania, dismantled, transported to Key Largo, and reassembled on

the reef. A lighthouse keeper and his family lived on the light, along with an assistant, coping with hardships such as Indian attacks when they went ashore. In the early 1900s Carysfort Lighthouse was rumored to be haunted by the ghost of Captain Johnson, a former lighthouse keeper who died there. The mysterious groaning attributed to Captain Johnson was later thought to be the result of the iron walls of the tower cooling at night. The lighthouse still operates on the reef today, although it has been unmanned since 1960.

Carysfort's combination of very shallow elkhorn coral and deep spurs of reef-building corals, such as star and

A. *Carysfort Reef is marked by Carysfort Lighthouse, which was built in 1852 and is 112 feet (34 meters) tall. The lighthouse has recently been restored and is used as a research station; it still functions as a navigation aid, but the light mechanism has been automated. The reef surrounding the light is excellent for both diving and snorkeling.*

B. *The large areas of shallow elkhorn coral,* Acropora palmata, *at Carysfort Reef are great for diving or snorkeling.*

C. *The largest colonies of elkhorn coral and staghorn coral,* Acropora cervicornis, *in the Florida Keys grow on Carysfort and South Carysfort Reefs.*

D. *A foureye butterflyfish,* Chaetodon capistratus, *swims among the branches of staghorn coral at Carysfort Reef.*

E. *A diver examines the colonies of elkhorn coral that grow on Carysfort Reef.*

brain coral, makes it an excellent reef for both diving and snorkeling.

Carysfort Reef is located 5.5 nautical miles (10.1 kilometers) off the northern end of Key Largo. The seaward side of the reef has an unusual double spur-and-groove system. The shallower system is covered with living coral, but there is also a deeper system of fossil coral. The shoreward side of the reef is well protected from waves, making it an excellent snorkeling site. The depths range from the surface to 80 feet (24.3 meters). Visibility is normally 40 to 60 feet (12.2 to 18.2 meters), with greater visibility when the Gulf Stream brings blue water in to the reef line. Carysfort Reef is included within a Sanctuary Preservation Area, with strict regulations against damage to the coral by divers and anchors. Fishing and lobstering are also prohibited here.

F. A school of Atlantic spadefish, Chaeto-dipterus faber, *entertain a diver at Carysfort Reef.*

G. This queen angel-fish, Holacanthus ciliaris, *is swimming in about 30 feet (9 meters) of water on South Carysfort Reef.*

H. Caribbean reef squid, Sepioteuthis sepioidea, *can be observed at night at the back of Carysfort Reef.*

South Carysfort Reef

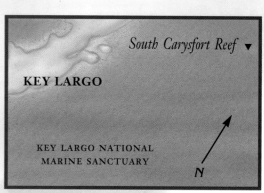

KEY LARGO

South Carysfort Reef ▼

KEY LARGO NATIONAL
MARINE SANCTUARY

N

GULF OF MEXICO

FLORIDA

Key Largo

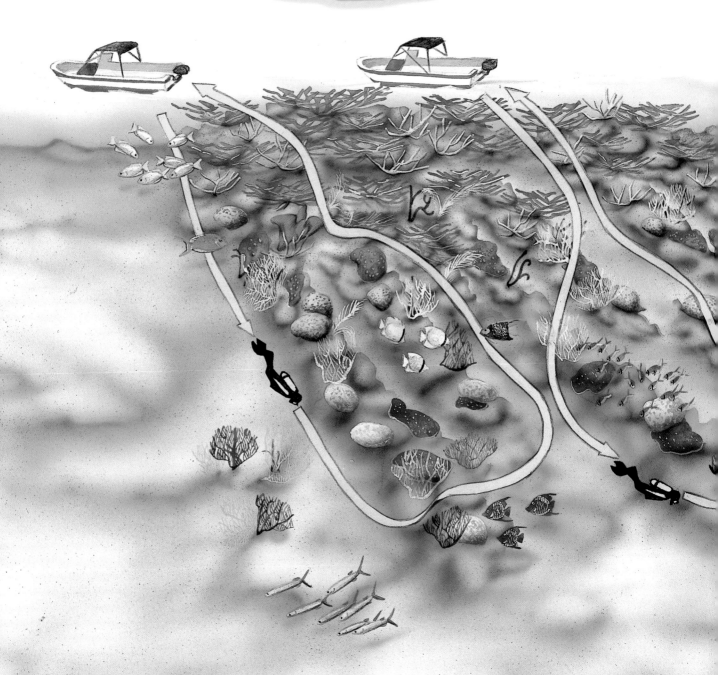

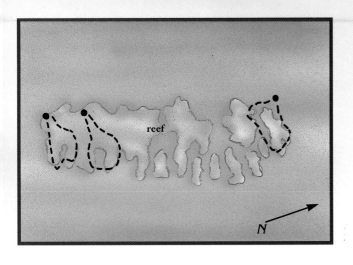

reef

N

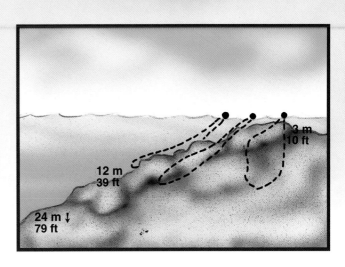

3 m
10 ft

12 m
39 ft

24 m ↓
79 ft

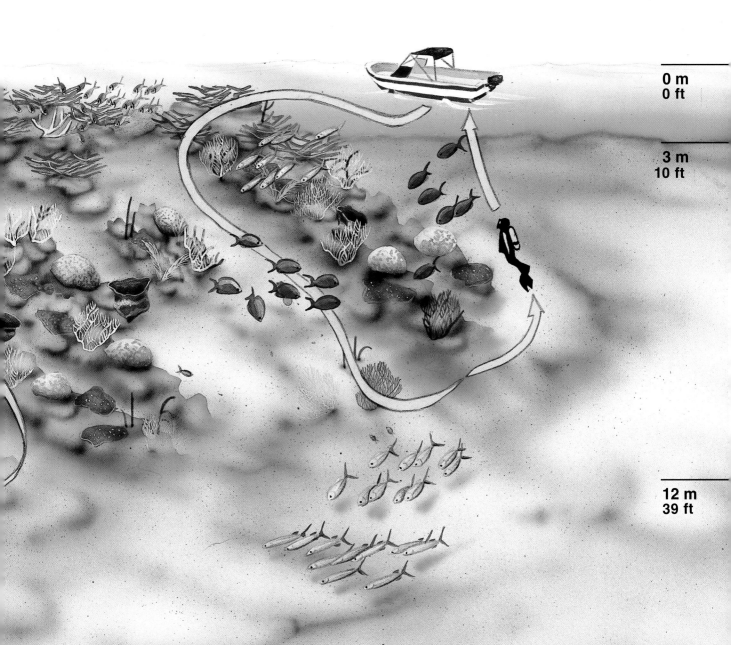

0 m
0 ft

3 m
10 ft

12 m
39 ft

24 m ↓
79 ft

A. A stoplight parrot-fish, Sparisoma viride, *about to settle in for the night next to a barrel sponge,* Xestospongia muta, *on the edge of South Carysfort Reef.*

B. A diver observes an enormous boulder brain coral, Colpophylia natans, *which must have been growing for many decades.*

Although it is not marked with a lighthouse like Carysfort Reef, South Carysfort Reef is also a large, shallow reef with elkhorn coral along the entire reef crest, giving way to boulders of star coral and brain coral in deeper water. The coral ridges that make up the spur-and-groove system run from about 10 to 40 feet (3 to 12.2 meters), rising as high as 15 feet (4.6 meters) from the bottom. They generally get lower in profile as they get deeper, until they are only 1 or 2 feet

A

C

D

C. Extra care should be taken around leafy fire coral to avoid stings on bare skin.

D. Juvenile fish often have very different colors from those of adults. Here is a French angelfish, Pomacanthus paru, *one of the many juvenile fish that can be seen on South Carysfort Reef.*

(30 to 60 centimeters) high in 50 or 60 feet (15.2 to 18.2 meters) of water. The boulder corals are gradually replaced by encrusting corals and barrel sponges in these deeper sections of the reef.

Schools of blue surgeonfish can usually be seen cruising the reef, stopping en masse to feed for a minute then moving on as though some signal had been given. Among the branches of elkhorn coral, bicolor damselfish cultivate patches of algae as their personal gardens, fiercely defending them against intruders.

Even divers will find their hands being nipped by these tiny fish if they approach too closely. Another fish family that you are certain to see here are the parrotfishes, including colorful stoplight parrotfish, large midnight parrotfish, and blue parrotfish. Parrot-fish nibble at the coral, digesting the coral polyps and excreting the calcium carbonate skeleton as sand.

South Carysfort reef is located 5.5 nautical miles (10.1 kilometers) off the northern end of Key Largo, about

E. Giant star coral polyps, Montastrea cavernosa, *are among the reef-building hard corals. Symbiotic algae called zooxanthellae greatly increase the reef-building capacity of such hard corals.*

F. A sponge brittle star, Ophiothrix suensonii, *crawls along a sponge at night on the deeper section of South Carysfort Reef.*

G. This spotfin butterflyfish, Chaetodon ocellatus, *in nighttime coloration, is probably eating the coral polyps.*

1 mile (1.6 kilometers) south of Carysfort Reef. Depths range from the surface to about 80 feet (24.3 meters). The reef crest on all sides is excellent for snorkeling, with some of the most pristine elkhorn and staghorn corals in the entire Florida Keys. When the trade winds are blowing from their usual northeast direction, the water is smoother on the shoreward side of the reef. Visibility is normally 40 to 60 feet (12.2 to 18.2 meters), with greater visibility when the Gulf

G

E

H

F

I

Stream brings blue water in to the reef line.

South Carysfort Reef is a Sanctuary Preservation Area, with the same strict regulations against damage to the coral by divers and anchors that apply at Carysfort Reef. Fishing and lobstering are prohibited at South Carysfort.

H. Glasseye snapper, Priacanthus cruentatus, *can often be observed in the shelter of an undercut ledge on South Carysfort Reef.*

I. A close-up of a balloonfish, Diodon holocanthus.

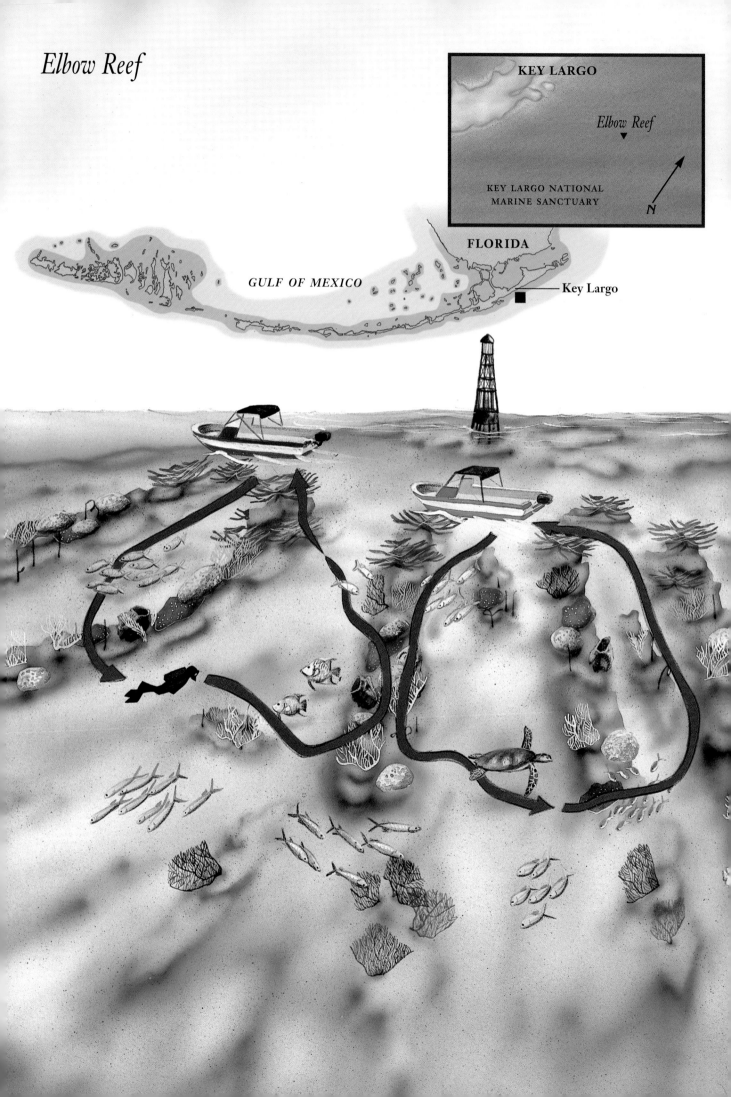

Elbow Reef

KEY LARGO

Elbow Reef

KEY LARGO NATIONAL
MARINE SANCTUARY

N

FLORIDA

GULF OF MEXICO

Key Largo

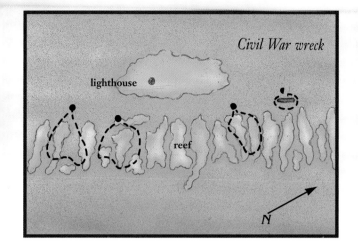

Civil War wreck

lighthouse

reef

N

6 m
20 ft

4.5 m
15 ft

15 m
49 ft

27 m↓
89 ft

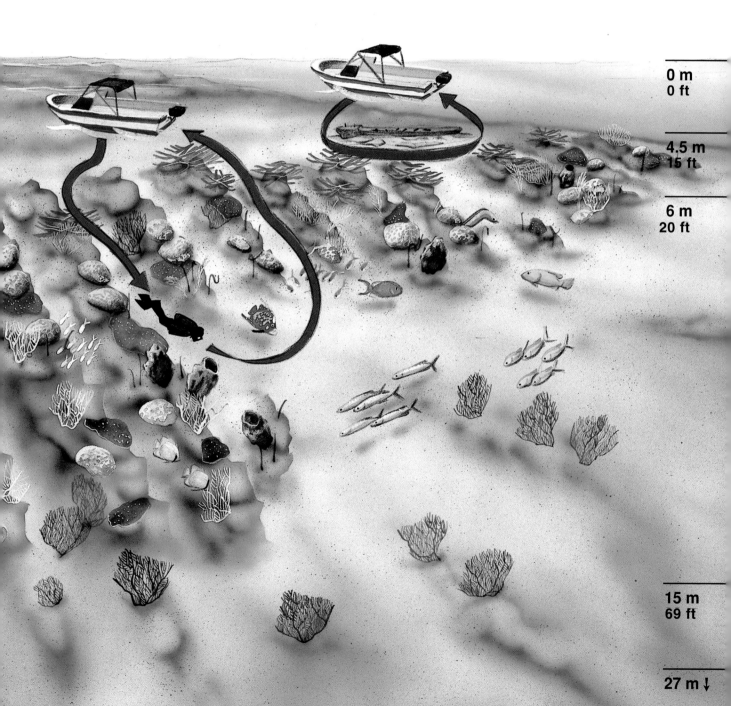

0 m
0 ft

4.5 m
15 ft

6 m
20 ft

15 m
69 ft

27 m ↓

A

A. The Civil War wreck, a wooden vessel that sank on the Elbow in the 1860s, is always a good place to dive. The exposed timbers and metal fasteners are visible here.

B. Closely packed schools of snappers and grunts swim the Civil War wreck.

C. A diver examines the exposed and encrusted timbers of the Civil War wreck.

D. Schools of snappers and grunts look for protection close to the Civil War wreck.

B

C

This reef takes its name from the fact that it sticks out slightly from the other reefs, like an elbow on a bent arm. That bit of geographical serendipity is the good fortune of Elbow Reef, because it means that the clear blue waters of the Gulf Stream are present here more often than at almost any other reef in the Florida Keys. Visibility at the Elbow is nearly always excellent.

As with other outer bank reefs, the Elbow's principal formations are the spur and groove. The tops of the spurs are covered with live coral, including elkhorn, star coral, smooth brain coral, convoluted brain coral, and giant star coral. The soft corals are represented

D

by sea fans, sea plumes, and sea rods, which thrive in the clear water.

Sea life is always prolific at the Elbow. For some reason sea turtles are often seen here, and it is not unusual for divers to suddenly become aware of a green or hawksbill turtle looking curiously over their shoulders. Green moray eels are also common at the Elbow, usually coiled within the coral crevices with only their heads showing. Barracuda, rays, and jacks are among the predatory fish common here.

You may come across the remains of several ships on the Elbow, including the *Tonawanda* and the Civil War wreck. Both of these consist of scattered remains, with only portions of the hulls

E

from 15 to 90 feet (4.6 to 27.4 meters), with much of the live coral between 20 and 50 feet (6 and 15.2 meters). The Elbow receives little protection from waves, owing to its position farther seaward than other reefs; however, the excellent visibility and fish life make snorkeling good. Visibility is normally 50 to 80 feet (15.2 to 24.3 meters).

The Elbow Reef is a designated Sanctuary Preservation Area, which has strict regulations against damage to coral by divers and boaters. Fishing and lobstering are not allowed.

E. The Elbow's coral ridges, clear water, and plentiful reef fish make it a favorite for divers.

F. A mixed school of grunts finds shelter within the exposed timbers of the Civil War wreck on the Elbow.

G. The extraordinary life forms growing on the Civil War wreck on the Elbow are subjects of impressive photographs.

H. This diver enjoys a face-to-face encounter with a spotted moray eel, Gymnothorax moringa, *on the Civil War wreck.*

F

G

intact. The *Tonawanda* is a metal steamer that sank in 1866, while the Civil War wreck is somewhat older and consists of wooden beams and metal fasteners. Fish are always thick at either site, even though they are fairly well deteriorated. The Civil War wreck is a particular favorite with photographers because the fish are so cooperative. Cottonwicks, French grunts, and squirrelfish are packed into the remains of the vessel, peering out for the lens. The more patient and still you are, the closer they will let you approach.

The Elbow is located about 5 miles (8 kilometers) off the central part of Key Largo, marked by a lighted tower with open tubular construction. Depths range

H

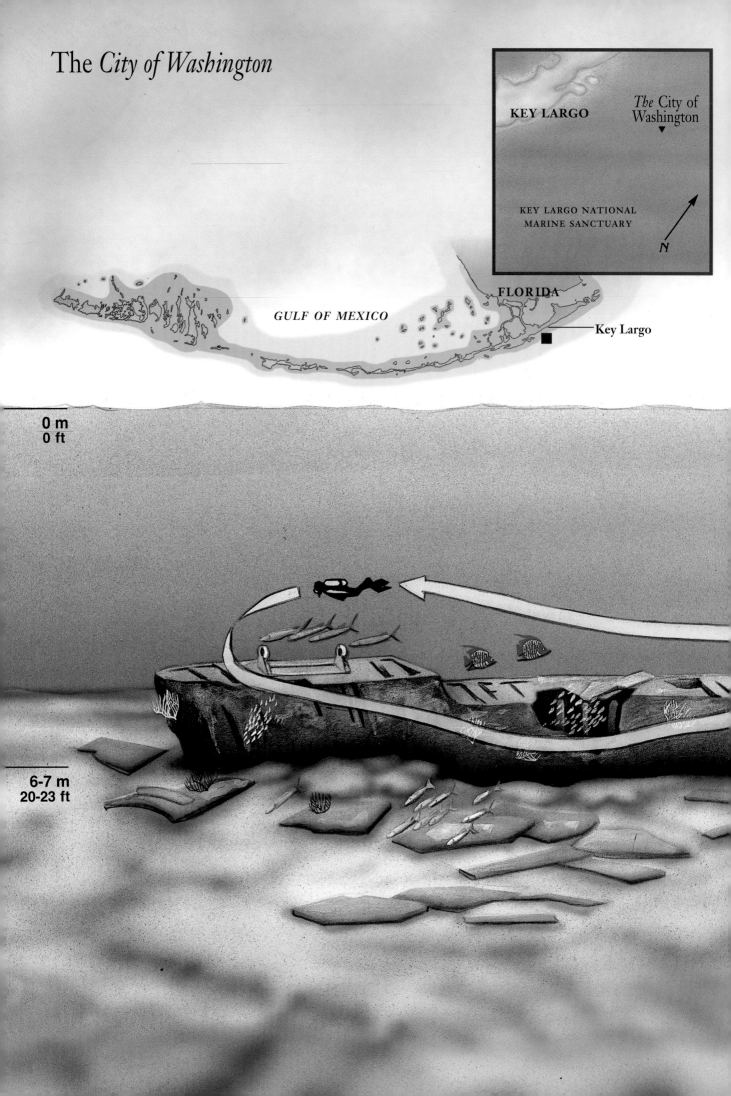

The *City of Washington*

KEY LARGO

The City of Washington

KEY LARGO NATIONAL
MARINE SANCTUARY

N

FLORIDA

GULF OF MEXICO

Key Largo

0 m
0 ft

6-7 m
20-23 ft

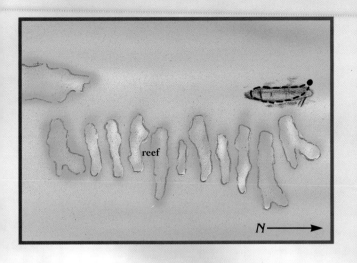

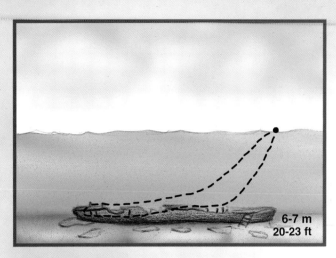

6-7 m
20-23 ft

Sunk on Elbow Reef on July 10, 1917, this former passenger liner and troopship is being reclaimed by the sea as the years pass. The *City of Washington* was built in 1877 by the shipyard of John Roach and Sons in Pennsylvania. Constructed of iron, the hull was 320 feet (97.5 meters) long with a beam of 38 feet (11.6 meters). She looked like a steamship, but was fitted with 3 masts and carried sails to supplement the power of her 3-cylinder engines. The *City of Washington* had a brief moment of glory in 1858, on an evening when she was anchored peacefully next to the battleship *Maine* in Havana Harbor. When the *Maine* suddenly exploded, the crew of the *City of*

Washington launched their lifeboats and rescued 90 crew. The *City of Washington* was struck by shrapnel from *Maine*'s explosion, putting several of the lifeboats out of commission.

For the next 10 years the *City of Washington* continued to carry passengers between New York and Cuba. In 1908 she was converted to a coal barge. Her engines and superstructure were removed, but her masts were retained even though she was not capable of sailing under her own power. In 1917 she ran aground at Elbow Reef while under tow by the tug *Edgar F. Luckenbach* and sank.

Today only the outline of the decks remains, along with a huge tangle of

A. Wreckage of a steel-hulled ship, the City of Washington, *320 feet (98 meters) long, that sank in 1917.*

B. It can be an emotional experience for divers to discover the story of ships that traveled these waters long ago.

C. Banded butterfly-fish, Chaetodon striatus, *can be seen particularly at night.*

D. A diver encounters a friendly green moray eel, Gymnothorax funebris, *on the* City of Washington.

steel that provides shelter for a host of creatures. Slabs of metal from the hull still stick up from the bottom, and the plates form lots of cracks and crevices. Most of the wreck is well decorated with many hard and soft corals on the top surfaces and colorful encrusting sponges underneath. Two big green moray eels live here and have become accustomed to the presence of divers. They can provide the most amazing photographic opportunities when you are lucky enough to find them out of their lairs. If they approach you, stay calm and do not wave your hands. Nurse sharks and great barracuda are also seen regularly on the wreck and may follow you around during the dive.

The wreck lies in only 20 to 25 feet (6 to 7.6 meters) of water on the northern side of the reef, where the currents are generally not strong. Visibility is normally 50 to 80 feet (15.2 to 24.3 meters). In addition to the wreck itself, the surrounding reef area is worth exploring. Remember that the Elbow Reef, including the *City of Washington*, is within a Sanctuary Preservation Area. Special prohibitions against damage to the coral have been implemented for this area and fishing is prohibited.

E

F

G

E. A succession of barracuda have been hand fed at the City of Washington, *a practice started years ago by Steve Klem and updated to "feeding by mouth" by Spencer Slate of the Atlantis Dive Center. Divers are likely to encounter these particularly bold fish on the wreck any time.*

F. The City of Washington *hosts many different kinds of fish. Here is a great barracuda,* Sphyraena barracuda.

G. The silver skin of this palometa, Trachinotus goodei, *swimming in the shallow water, reflects the light of the scuba diver's torch.*

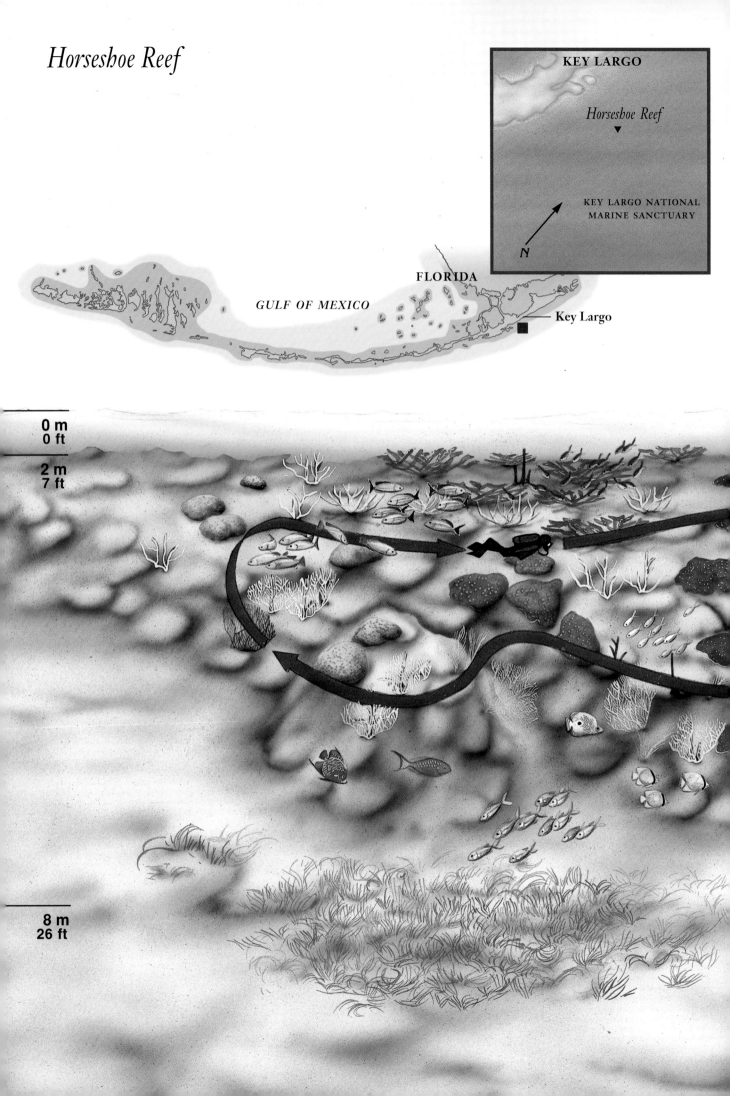

Horseshoe Reef

KEY LARGO

Horseshoe Reef

KEY LARGO NATIONAL
MARINE SANCTUARY

N

FLORIDA

GULF OF MEXICO

Key Largo

0 m
0 ft

2 m
7 ft

8 m
26 ft

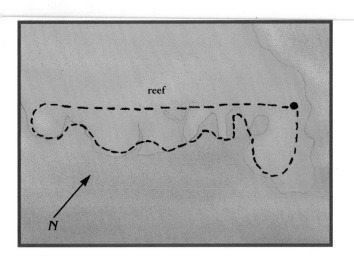

reef

N

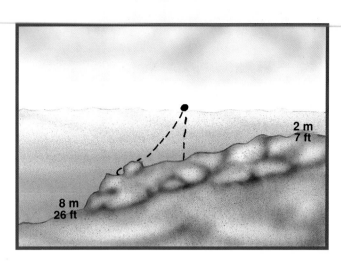

2 m
7 ft

8 m
26 ft

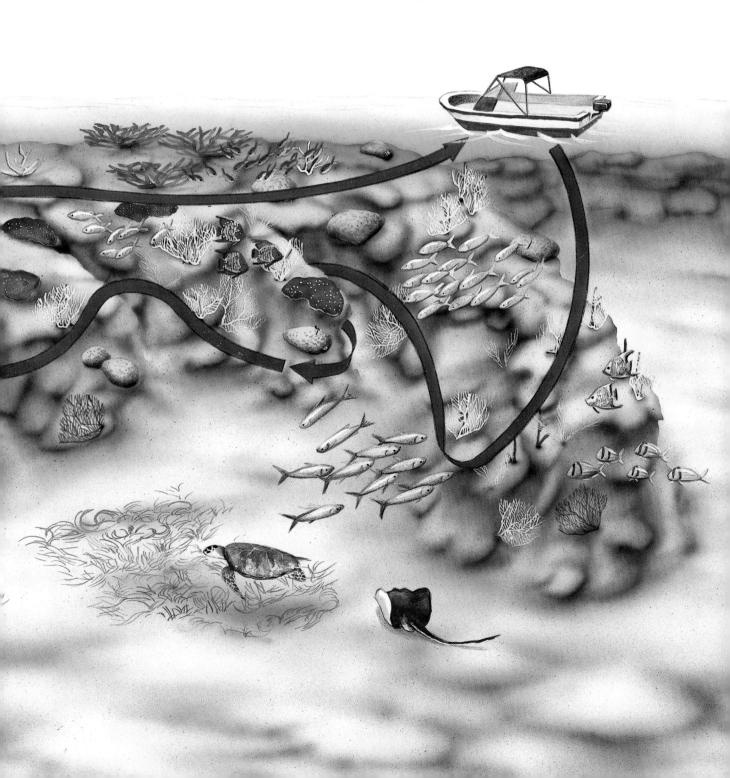

The depiction of this reef on the chart shows a crescent of shallow water that looks somewhat like a horseshoe, but any connection with either horses or shoes ends there. This reef is actually inshore of the other inner bank reefs, perched on the edge of Hawk Channel. The front side is like a mini-wall, 6 to 10 feet (1.8 to 3 meters) high and composed mostly of very large boulders of star coral. Some of these coral heads are more than 10 feet (3 meters) in diameter, which indicates an age of around 300 years at star coral's typical growth rate of less than .5 inch (1 centimeter) per year. Along the top of the reef are numerous smaller heads of brain and star coral.

B

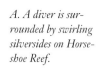

A

Elkhorn coral dominates the back side of the reef, rising to within 5 or 6 feet (1.5 to 1.8 meters) of the surface. Although all corals grow relatively slowly, elkhorn is one of the fastest-growing species. Whole colonies can migrate from one area of the reef to another in a few decades. This movement is apparent on Horseshoe Reef, where new growth of elkhorn can be seen adjacent to fossil coral.

This reef is excellent for fish watching and fish photography. The crevices are often filled with swirling schools of silversides, with marauding packs of black jacks flashing in to feed on them. Snappers, grunts, wrasses, and parrotfish are all found here.

C

D

A. A diver is surrounded by swirling silversides on Horseshoe Reef.

B. Bar jacks, Caranx ruber, *prey on a swirling school of silversides at Horseshoe Reef.*

C. The waters of Horseshoe Reef are renowned for the incredible numbers of schooling fish. Here is a school of smallmouth grunts, Haemulon chrysargyreum.

D. A diver is dwarfed by a huge colony of star coral, Montastrea annularis, *at Horseshoe Reef. This coral colony was already growing when the first shots of the American Revolution rang out.*

When the weather has been calm for a day or two, the visibility gets very good and the colors are spectacular. When the winds are up, the visibility goes down, but Horseshoe may still be a good choice because of its protected location close to shore. Do not ignore the sand flats and sea grass meadows seaward of the reef. These are good places to find helmet conch, tridents, southern stingrays, and green turtles. When you are swimming along the ledge on the seaward side of the reef, take the occasional short swim perpendicular to the reef for a minute or two and then come back. You may not see anything on these little jaunts across the sand, but when you do it will be worthwhile.

Horseshoe Reef is only 3.5 nautical miles (6.5 kilometers) offshore for the central portion of Key Largo. It lies about midway between the Elbow Reef and Key Largo Dry Rocks, but is closer to shore than either of those reefs. Depths on the reef range from 4 to 20 feet (1.2 to 6 meters). Like many of the inshore reefs, visibility depends on the weather, especially the wind. When the wind dies, the visibility increases. Visibility on Horseshoe Reef is normally 20 to 50 feet (6 to 15.2 meters), with higher visibility during calm weather.

E

F

G

E. This horse-eye jack, Caranx latus, is probably observing the photographer.

F. A southern stingray, Dasyatis americana, conceals itself in the sand on Horseshoe Reef.

G. Queen conch, Strombus gigas, are protected by law in the Keys area. This specimen has been photographed on one of the sandy areas at Horseshoe Reef.

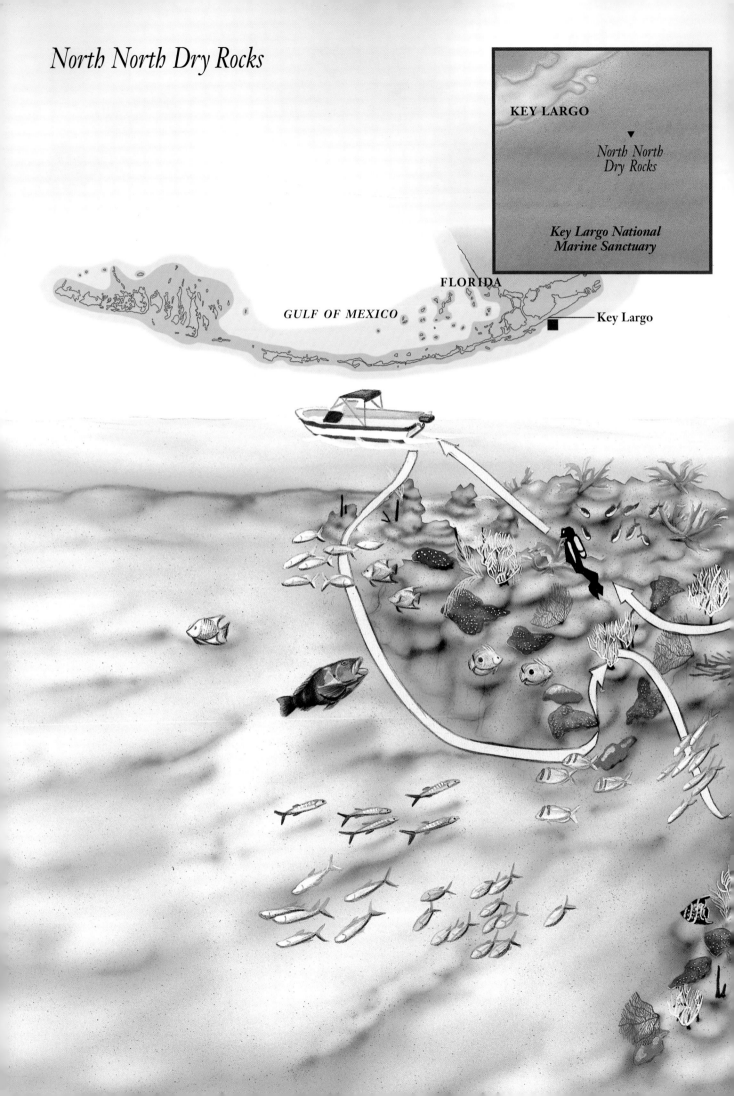

North North Dry Rocks

KEY LARGO

▼ North North Dry Rocks

Key Largo National Marine Sanctuary

FLORIDA

GULF OF MEXICO

Key Largo

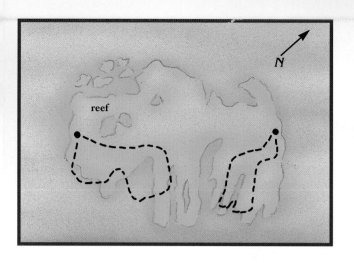

reef

N

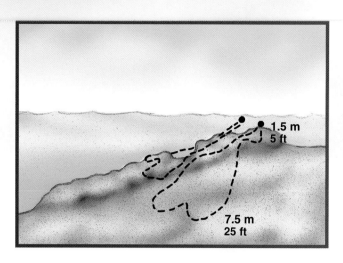

1.5 m
5 ft

7.5 m
25 ft

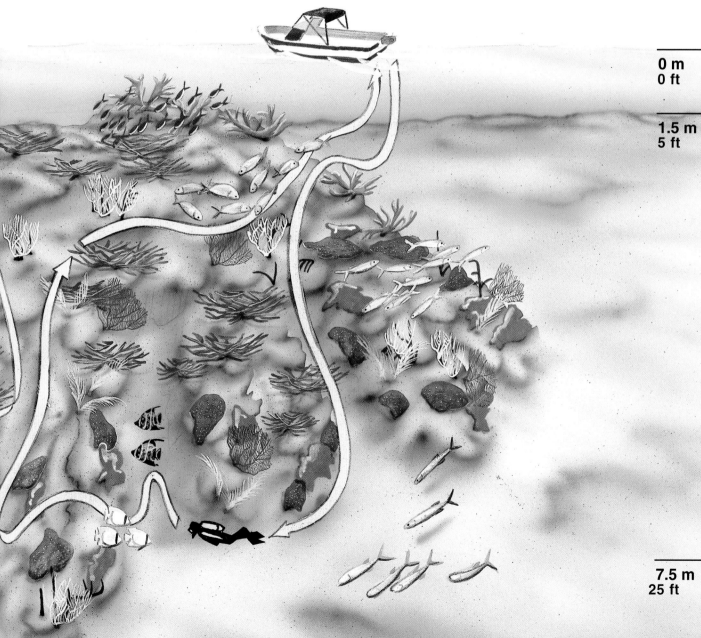

0 m
0 ft

1.5 m
5 ft

7.5 m
25 ft

N orth North Dry Rocks is, naturally, the first reef north of North Dry Rocks. Fortunately, there is no reef named North North North Dry Rocks, which could really be confusing. This is a wonderful reef for both diving and snorkeling. It is basically one big spur-and-groove formation. The spurs in this case are long and tall, undercut in numerous places with swim-throughs and ledges. The undersides of these ledges are encrusted with red, orange, and purple sponges. Golden brown thickets of elkhorn and staghorn coral can be found along the tops of the ridges. The sides are studded with spheres of knobby star coral and the smoother globes of starlet coral. The soft corals are also well represented by waving purple sea fans and brown sea rods. Here and there, sinuous sea plumes look like willow trees, swaying gently back and forth.

North North Dry Rocks is a fish watcher's delight and an excellent choice for both normal and macrophotography. On days when the underwater visibility is high, there are also many nice wide-angle photographic opportunities. Everything from tiny neon gobies and silversides to big Nassau groupers and great barracuda can be seen here. Look under ledges and within the branches of the thickest elkhorn formations for schools of copper sweepers. This pale-copper-colored fish can often be seen on North North Dry Rocks, swimming ceaselessly back and forth within the cover of the reef. Check for cleaning stations near large coral heads, too. Cleaner fish are small fish of several species that eat the external parasites on the skin and scales of other fish. Cleaners stay in one particular area on the reef, known as a cleaning station, and the customers come to them. You may see nearly any fish being cleaned, from small blue tangs to large black jacks. Several species of goby specialize in cleaning other fish, but it is often the juveniles of other species, especially Spanish hogfish and queen angelfish, who act as cleaners. The normal tendency of larger fish to eat smaller fish is temporarily suspended at cleaning stations. The fish to be cleaned even allows the cleaner to swim into its mouth and gill slits to strip away parasites.

North North Dry Rocks is located about 4 nautical miles (7.4 kilometers) off the central part of Key Largo, between the Elbow and Key Largo Dry Rocks. The depth range at North North Dry Rocks is from 4 to 25 feet (1.2 to 7.6 meters). Visibility usually ranges from 20 to 50 feet (6 to 15.2 meters). The position of the reef, slightly back from the outside of the reef, affords good protection.

D. Horse-eye jacks, Caranx latus, *schooling in the blue water on North North Dry Rocks.*

E. *A school of copper sweepers,* Pempheris schomburgki, *gathers among the branches of an elkhorn coral colony for protection from predators during the day.*

F. *A rock beauty,* Holacanthus tricolor, *searches for sponges, its favorite food, on North North Dry Rocks.*

G. *A Spanish lobster,* Scyllarides aequin-octialis, *at night on North North Dry Rocks.*

H. *The delicate colors of the Christmas tree worms enliven a hard coral formation.*

A. *A blue angelfish,* Holacanthus bermu-densis, *searches for food on the side of a coral-covered ridge at North North Dry Rocks.*

C. *A diver enjoys a close encounter with a curious Nassau grouper,* Epinephelus striatus, *on North North Dry Rocks.*

B. *The photographer's flash illuminates a multitude of swirling silversides in the depths of North North Dry Rocks.*

Key Largo Dry Rocks
(The Christ of the Abyss)

KEY LARGO

Key Largo
Dry Rocks

KEY LARGO NATIONAL
MARINE SANCTUARY

N

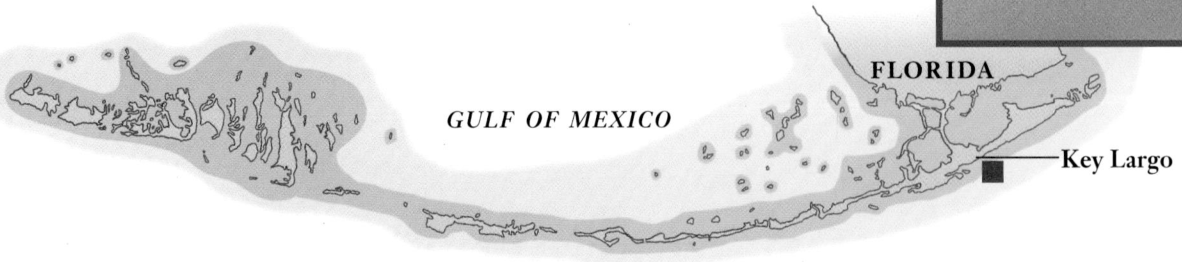

GULF OF MEXICO

FLORIDA

Key Largo

0 m
0 ft

3 m
10 ft

9 m
30 ft

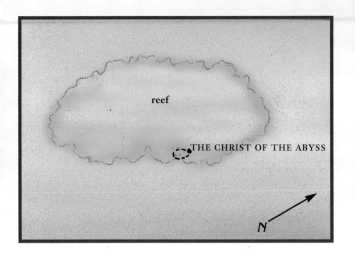

reef

THE CHRIST OF THE ABYSS

N

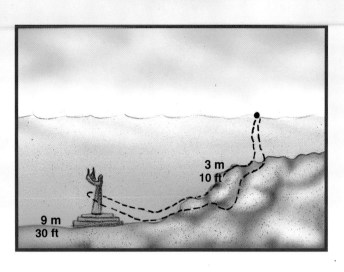

3 m
10 ft

9 m
30 ft

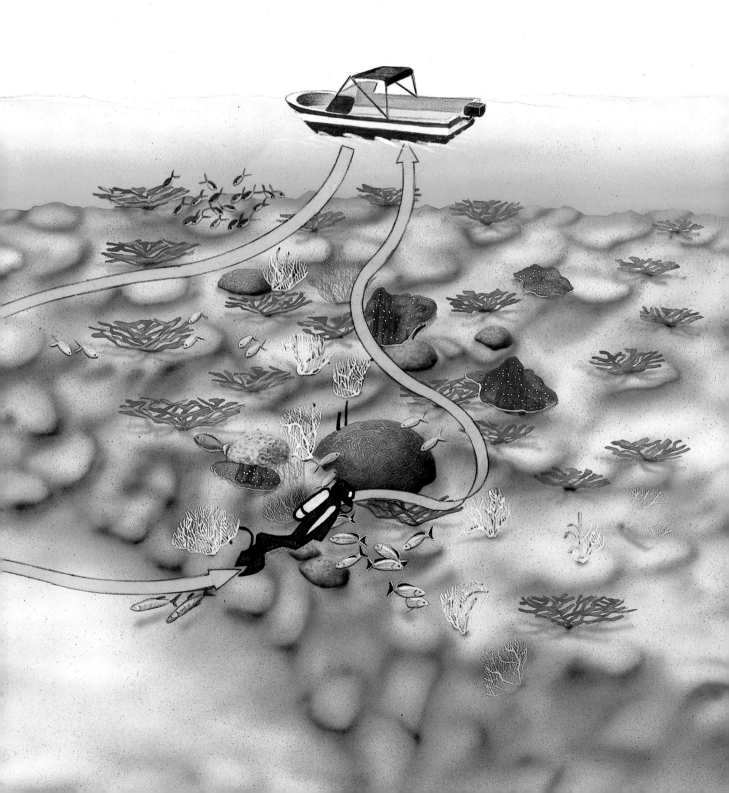

Key Largo Dry Rocks was supposed to be called Grecian Rocks, which is the name of another shallow reef less than 1 mile (1.6 kilometers) to the south. However, the 2 names were switched while being transcribed from an early chart, and the 2 reefs have had each other's names ever since. Key Largo Dry Rocks is an excellent example of an inner bank reef. It is located significantly closer to shore than the outer bank reefs and has some attributes of both outer bank reefs and patch reefs. On the seaward side is a truncated spur-and-groove formation; the top and back of the reef are shaped like a patch reef. Large boulders of star coral dominate the back side of the reef,

C

A

B

is easy to get temporarily lost. The coral is very dense on Key Largo Dry Rocks, making good buoyancy control very important.

The Christ of the Abyss statue is one of the most popular attractions on Key Largo Dry Rocks. Nestled on a concrete pedestal in the sand between 2 tall coral spurs, this 9-foot (2.7-meter) bronze statue of Jesus greets the sun with open arms. Originally presented to the Underwater Society of America in 1962 by dive gear manufacturer Egidio Cressi, it was destined to take a 4-year odyssey from Chicago to Orlando to St. Petersburg before reaching the Florida Keys. Through the perseverance of Ellison Hardee, the first superintendent

D

spilling out onto the sand as though they had been stacked up once and somehow tumbled down. The entire reef is surrounded by sand and sea grass, about 30 feet (9 meters) deep in front and 10 feet (3 meters) deep in back. The thick elkhorn coral on top of the reef has 2 or 3 feet (0.6 or 0.9 meters) of water over it at high tide and less than 1 foot (30 centimeters) at low tide.

Key Largo Dry Rocks can be dived and snorkeled even when bad weather has made most of the other reefs uncomfortable, although water clarity may suffer in a rough sea. This is a fabulous dive on a good day. Even though the reef is circular, there are so many coral ravines and alleyways that it

of Pennekamp Park, the 4,000-pound (1,814-kilogram) statue was placed on the Key Largo Dry Rocks reef in 1966. This statue is actually the third cast from the same mold. An identical Christ of the Abyss statue was placed in 50 feet (15.2 meters) of water in the Gulf of Genoa off San Fruttuoso, Italy, in 1954. In 1961, the second statue was erected overlooking St. George's harbor in Grenada. The Grenada statue commemorates the rescue of passengers and crew from the burning Italian liner *Bianca C.*, which later sank outside the harbor.

Special care should be taken in the vicinity of the statue because it is such a popular attraction. Be aware of the boat

A. This enormous boulder brain coral, Colpophylia natans, *has been growing for many decades near the Christ of the Abyss statue on Key Largo Dry Rocks.*

B. The Christ of the Abyss statue, placed underwater at Key Largo Dry Rocks in 1966, is in 15 feet (4.5 meters) of water. An identical statue is in 50 feet (15 meters) of water off San Fruttuoso, Italy.

C. The Christ of the Abyss statue is almost always surrounded by many fish, including these yellowtail snappers, Ocyurus chrysurus.

D. The statue is one of the most popular dive and snorkel sites in the Keys. Underwater weddings are even performed here!

E. Snorkelers can easily see the thick colonies of elkhorn coral, Acropora palmata, *on the crest of Key Largo Dry Rocks. A boulder brain coral,* Colpophylia natans, *is in the foreground.*

F. The sun rays filter through the clear water of Dry Rocks and illuminate the statue of the Christ of the Abyss.

G. A diver closely examines the statue; this dive is quite easy and is a good example of an inner bank reef dive.

traffic in the area. Although moorings are provided and boats maneuver slowly and cautiously, they do move frequently. Coral on the statue is another possible hazard. Like any other hard surface underwater, the statue is a good place for coral growth. In addition to some small colonies of star coral, the statue is encrusted in places with fire coral that can give a nasty sting. The statue also overlooks an enormous head of boulder brain coral. This formation is remarkable not only for its size and age, but for its unblemished health. Please avoid touching the brain coral to preserve it for future visitors.

The Christ of the Abyss has become a favorite location for an unlikely cere-

mony—underwater weddings. Upward of 200 of these are performed here every year. Some are quite simple, but others are lavish productions that rival normal topside ceremonies.

Key Largo Dry Rocks is located about 4 nautical miles (7.4 kilometers) offshore of the central part of Key Largo. Depths range from the surface to 30 feet (9 meters). Visibility normally ranges from 25 to 50 feet (7.6 to 15.2 meters), depending on the weather. Key Largo Dry Rocks has been designated as a Sanctuary Preservation Area, so be extra cautious to avoid any type of damage to the coral. Fishing by any means is prohibited on and around this reef.

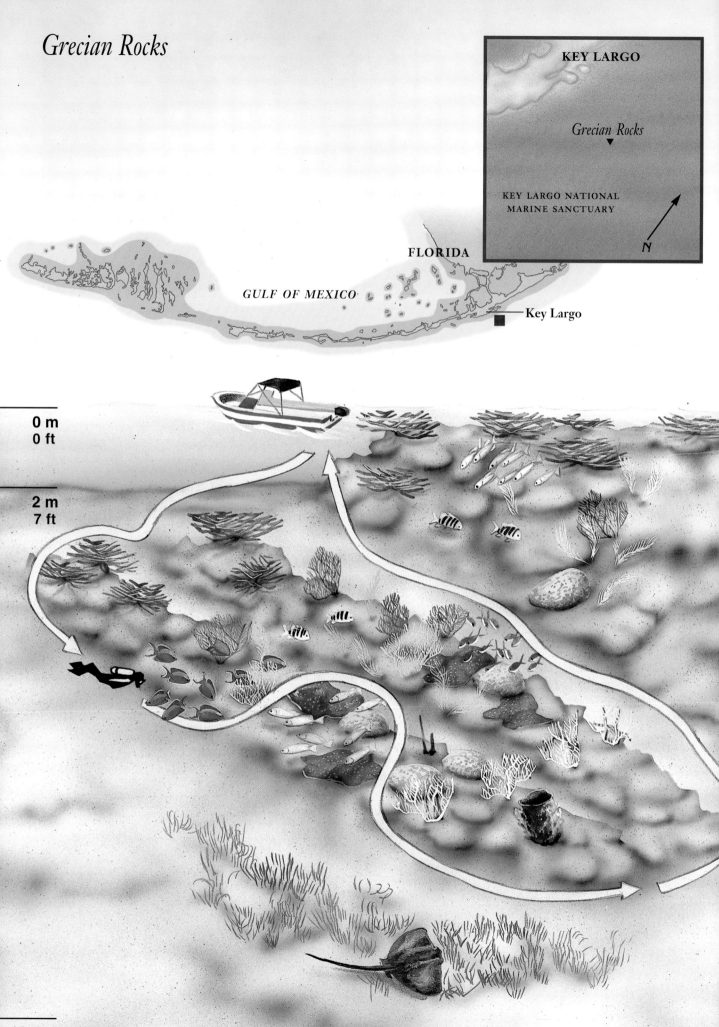

Grecian Rocks

KEY LARGO

Grecian Rocks ▾

KEY LARGO NATIONAL
MARINE SANCTUARY

N

FLORIDA

GULF OF MEXICO

Key Largo

0 m
0 ft

2 m
7 ft

10.5 m
34 ft

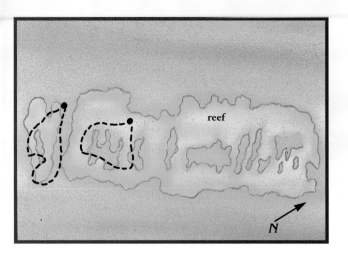

reef

N

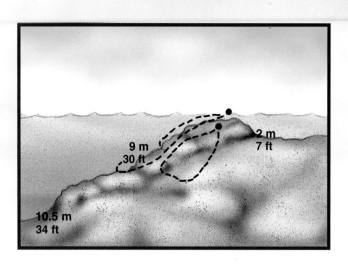

9 m
30 ft

2 m
7 ft

10.5 m
34 ft

A

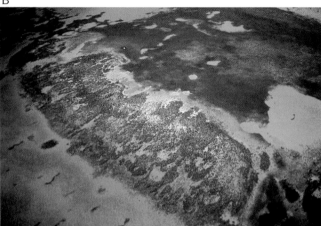

B

C

Grecian Rocks is one of the most unusual reefs in the Upper Keys. The fore reef is long and well-developed like the outer bank reefs, but it is set back a considerable distance from the outer reefs. The reef crest is the shallowest of all the Upper Keys reefs, with large portions of the reef showing at low tide. The back reef is long and broad, almost like a sandy plateau behind the reef crest. There is a bare sand band adjacent to the reef, but a thick gloss of turtle grass covers the rest of the plateau. The water behind the reef is very shallow, only 3 to 6 feet (1 to 2 meters) depending on the state of the tide. These characteristics make Grecian Rocks a good choice when the weather is not cooperating, because the

A and B. These aerial views of Grecian Rocks show the shallow back reef with sand and sea grass, the extremely shallow reef crest, and the fore reef with coral spurs and sandy grooves.

C. On the sandy flat behind Grecian Rocks you can see curious animals, such as this cushion sea star, Oreaster reticulatus.

D

shallow reef crest provides an effective lee. When the wind is up, Grecian Rocks has good conditions longer than any other reef. The structure of Grecian Rocks also makes it excellent for both diving and snorkeling. The front side of the reef is a truncated but highly developed spur-and-groove system with good coral cover. Toward the reef crest the spurs are topped with elkhorn coral.

As the depth increases, the branching corals give way to boulders of star, giant star, starlet, and brain coral. Everywhere on the front of the reef there are sea fans, sea rods, and sea plumes.

The back of the reef is more suited for snorkeling, owing to its shallow depth. Along the reef edge and across the sand to the sea grass, there are many different species of reef fish. Most of the Florida Keys parrotfish species

D. This midnight parrotfish, Scarus coelestinus, was photographed on the front side of Grecian Rocks at night.

E. Spiny lobsters, Panulirus argus, can often be observed during dives on Grecian Rocks.

F. Elkhorn coral, Acropora palmata, characterizes the reef crest at Grecian Rocks.

G. Many divers are unaware of the importance of the sea grass beds, which stabilize the bottom and prevent harmful sedimentation. They also provide habitats and food for many creatures, including this queen conch, Strombus gigas, grazing in the turtle grass.

H. Soft corals have a flexible skeleton, unlike the brittle skeleton of calcium carbonate in hard corals. Soft corals are generally referred to as "octocorals" because each polyp has 8 tentacles; most hard corals have only 6.

E

F

G

can be seen at times in the shallows behind the reef, including stoplight, princess, queen, and blue parrotfish. Watching fish here is like standing on a busy street corner—there is a constant flow of different fish back and forth. This is also an excellent place to see queen conch making their way across the sea grass. Conch are protected in the Sanctuary Preservation Area.

Grecian Rocks is located about 5 nautical miles (9.3 kilometers) from Key Largo, between Key Largo Dry Rocks and the *Benwood* wreck. Depths range from the surface to about 35 feet (10.6 meters) on the front side of the reef. Visibility normally ranges from 25 to 50 feet (7.6 to 15.2 meters) depending on the weather. Currents

H

are not usually strong. Divers should take extra care not to touch the coral at Grecian Rocks; it is included within a Sanctuary Preservation Area with strict regulations against damage to the coral.

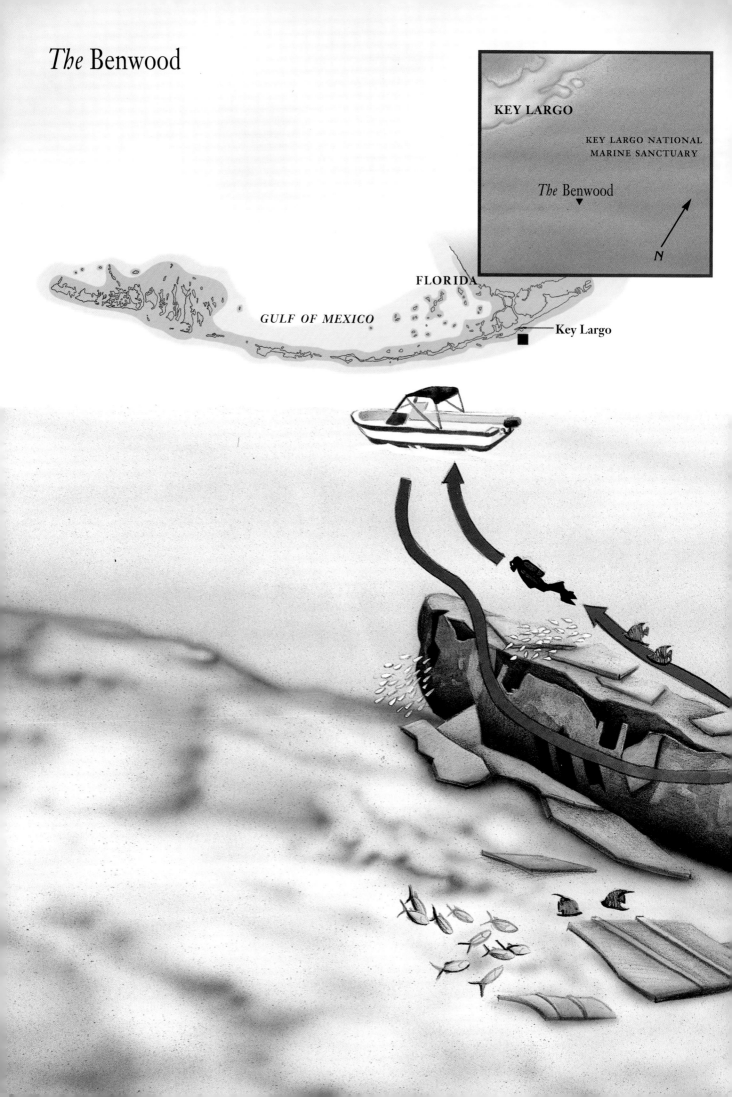

The Benwood

KEY LARGO

KEY LARGO NATIONAL
MARINE SANCTUARY

The Benwood

N

FLORIDA

GULF OF MEXICO

Key Largo

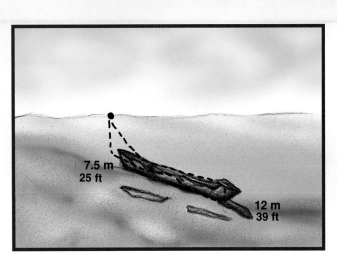

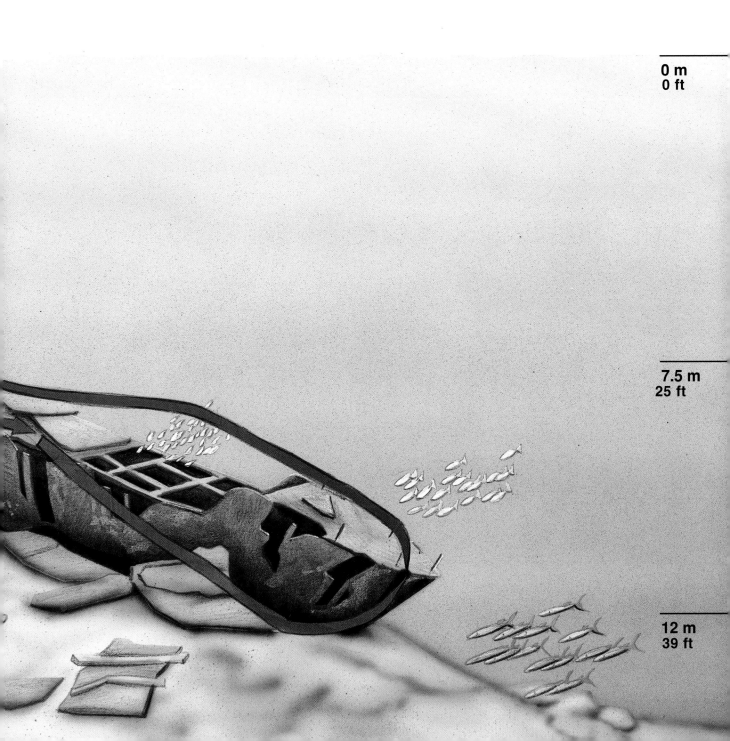

0 m
0 ft

7.5 m
25 ft

12 m
39 ft

A

B

C

The wreck of the *Benwood* tells a true saga from World War II; however, visitors are likely to hear many different versions of the story from dive masters in the Florida Keys. The *Benwood*, built in England in 1910, was 360 feet (109.7 meters) long with a beam of 51 feet (15.5 meters). She left Tampa, Florida on April 6, 1942, loaded with phosphate rock, as part of the Allied wartime fleet of freighters. The *Benwood* was supposed to swing around the southern tip of Florida, staying 3 miles (5 kilometers) off the Florida Keys reefs, en route to Norfolk, Virginia, with a final destination of Liverpool, England. This is where the story gets interesting.

A. The crumpled bow of the Benwood, *the result of a collision with the tanker Robert C. Tuttle.*

B. A mixed school of reef fish find shelter along the steel hull of the Benwood.

C. A gray angelfish, Pomacanthus arcuatus, *swims near the bow of the* Benwood.

D. This aerial view shows the Benwood *wreck with two dive boats moored on it.*

D

The *Benwood* was running without lights, owing to the strong possibility of attack by German submarines. Also running without lights was the 544-foot (166-meter) tanker *Robert C. Tuttle*, which was headed in the opposite direction. The *Tuttle* was supposed to be moving south one and a half miles (2.4 kilometers) from the reefs. Both vessels, however, were off their prescribed courses. At about 1 A.M. lookouts on the *Benwood* finally saw the *Tuttle*, very close to the *Benwood*'s starboard bow. The *Benwood* turned hard to port about the same time the *Tuttle* saw her and turned hard to starboard. The inevitable collision smashed the *Benwood*'s bow, dooming the struggling freighter. The captain tried to beach the vessel, but was unable to maneuver sufficiently. The *Benwood* sank on the outer line of the reef about 7 miles (11.3 kilometers) south of the Elbow.

Many of the stories about the *Benwood* involve U-boats and torpedoes. One that is still being told has the *Benwood* colliding with the *Tuttle*, but then being torpedoed while limping back to port. There is no record of a German submarine torpedoing the *Benwood*, and the only damage seems to have come from the collision.

The *Benwood* rests upright on the bottom with the bow out to sea. Much of the structure has been removed or collapsed, but the forward section is relatively intact and the smashed bow is clearly visible. The depth is about 25 feet (7.6 meters) near the stern and 40 feet (12.2 meters) at the bow. Four mooring buoys have been installed on the *Benwood*.

The *Benwood* is a bit too deep for snorkeling but perfect for scuba diving. The metal beams and slab sides of the hull have created extensive habitats for hundreds of reef fish. A variety of species school next to the metal during the day, including schoolmasters, yellow goatfish, bluestriped grunts, porkfish, and cottonwicks. Queen, gray, and French angelfish pick at the encrusting sponges, and stoplight parrotfish nibble on the coral polyps.

The *Benwood* is a popular night dive, too. The wreck is not too deep, so access from Key Largo is fairly straightforward at night. Navigation on the *Benwood* at night is relatively easy, especially when you are familiar with the wreck from a previous day dive. The colors of the sponges and corals come alive under the beam of your dive light.

The *Benwood* is located just under 5 nautical miles (9.3 kilometers) offshore, almost on a line between the Elbow and Molasses Reef. Depth ranges from 20 to 45 feet (6 to 13.7 meters) and visibility is usually 30 to 70 feet (9 to 21.3 meters).

E. *Yellow goatfish,* Mulloidichthys martinicus, *schooling near the wreckage of the* Benwood.

F. *The metal sides of the* Benwood *have become coated with coral and sponge since it sank after a collision in 1942.*

G. *The* Benwood *wreck attracts thousands of colorful reef fish, including the porkfish,* Anisotremus virginicus.

H. *A diver encounters a balloonfish,* Diodon holocanthus, *over the scattered wreckage at the stern of the* Benwood.

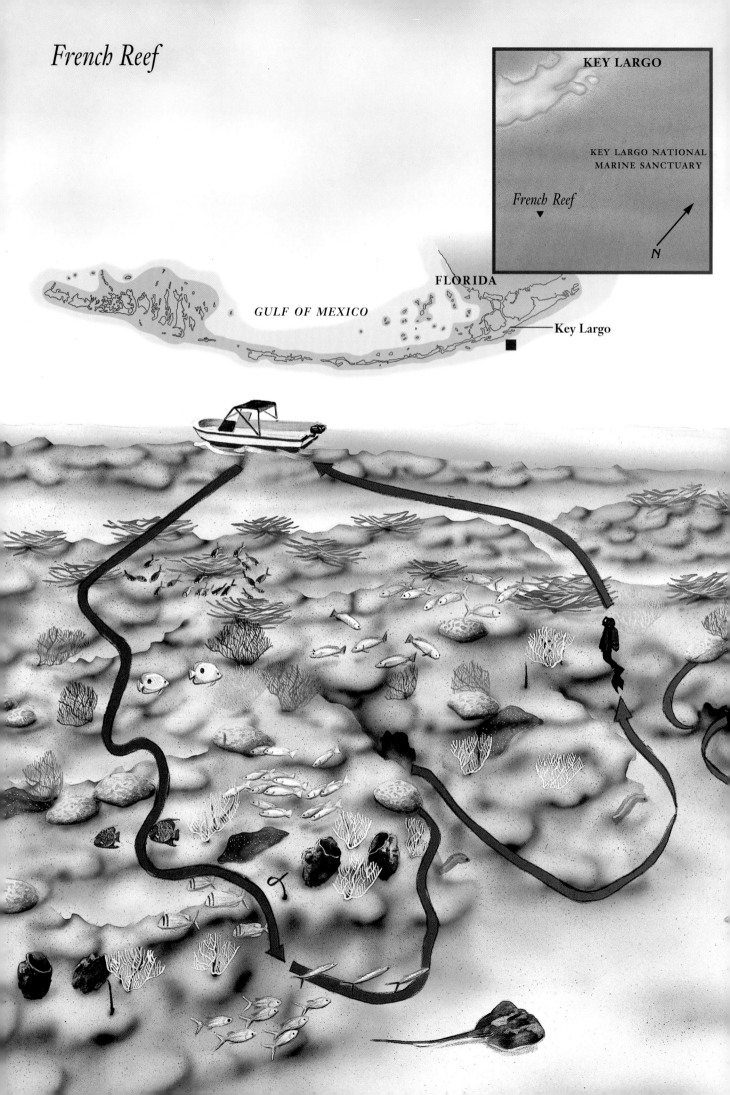

French Reef

KEY LARGO

KEY LARGO NATIONAL
MARINE SANCTUARY

French Reef

N

FLORIDA

GULF OF MEXICO

Key Largo

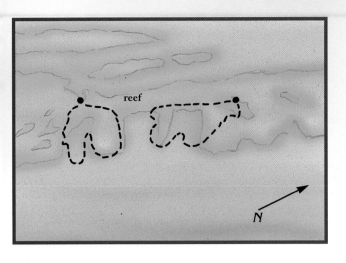

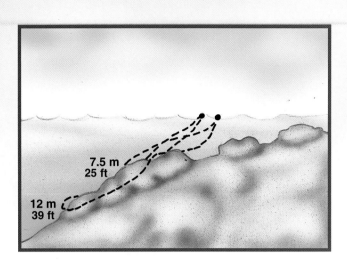

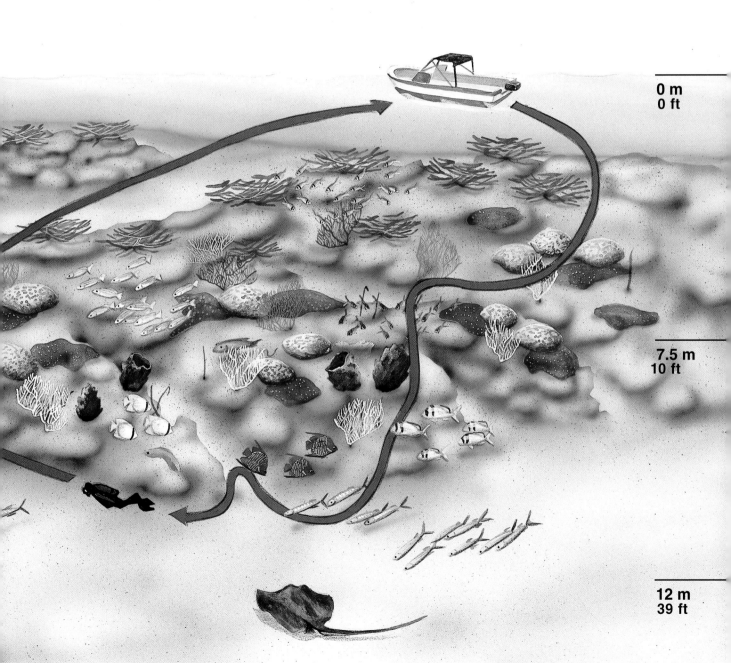

The usual orderly rows of coral spurs and sand channels have been modified by time into a labyrinth of coral walls on French Reef. The coral ridges turn back on themselves here, forming a series of interesting pockets, caves, and swim-throughs. In the shallower reef areas, the ridges are topped with golden brown stands of elkhorn coral, one of the fastest growing of the hard corals. As the depth increases, boulders of brain coral and star coral begin to dominate. Between about 30 and 40 feet (9.2 and 12.2 meters) there is a series of large, ancient coral mounds. The myriad nooks and crevices and the extent of live coral on French Reef make this a

C

A

D

B

favorable habitat for hundreds of fish species. Divers are likely to see schools of many different parrotfish, grunts, jacks, and damselfish, as well as larger solitary fish such as snook, permit, and barracuda. The caves formed under the coral ridges are not dangerously deep or long, but should be entered carefully to avoid damage to the coral. Under-water navigation is challenging on French Reef because of the random coral structures. Divers often find themselves surfacing frequently to check the position of their boat. There are 4 sets of named caves at French Reef—Christmas Tree Cave, Hourglass Cave, White Sand Bottom Cave, and the Five Caves. All of the caves are located toward the southern end of the reef, at depths of 25 to 35 feet (7.6 to 10.7 meters). Christmas Tree Cave is named for the cone-shaped star coral formation that grows on the coral spur over the cave.

Christmas Tree Cave is only about 4 feet (1.2 meters) high, so it is cus-tomary to pull yourself through with your hands on the sandy bottom—swimming through stirs up the bottom for the next diver. Hourglass Cave is slightly wider than Christmas Tree Cave, but still somewhat low in height. The origin of the name becomes appar-ent when you see the coral column that divides the cave into 2 sections like an hourglass. White Sand Bottom Cave, located almost in the center of French Reef, is the largest and easiest to negotiate. A large, flat sandy patch is visible on either side of the cave.

A series of narrower caves at the south end of the reef is called Five Caves. These caves are either cul-de-sacs or small openings that are difficult to enter, so divers should not try to push into them. They are usually filled with fish such as copper sweepers, Atlantic spadefish, bluestriped grunts, and green moray eels. Approach the entrance carefully and shine a light inside to avoid spooking the fish.

French Reef is located about 5.5 nautical miles (10.1 kilometers) from Key Largo, between the *Benwood* wreck and Molasses Reef.

Depths at French Reef range from about 10 to 90 feet (3 to 27.4 meters). Currents usually vary from none to moderate, but can be strong on occasion. Visibility is normally 30 to 70 feet (92 to 21.3 meters).

A curious anomaly in the ebb and flow of water across the reefs often bathes French Reef in green water while nearby Molasses Reef is in blue water. In these conditions you can see a distinct line where the water color changes from blue to green between French and Molasses Reefs. Divers can often take advantage of this situation and choose between French and Molasses to find the least current or the best visibility.

French Reef is included within a Sanctuary Preservation Area, with strict regulations against damage to the coral by divers and anchors. Fishing and lobstering are also prohibited.

E

F

G

H

A. An underwater photographer with mixed schools of school-masters and Caesar grunts beneath elkhorn coral at French Reef.

B. Mixed schools of bluestriped grunts, Haemulon sciurus, *and yellow goatfish,* Mulloidichthys martinicus, *stay close to the coral at French Reef for protection.*

C. Atlantic spadefish, Chaetodipterus faber, *in about 40 feet (12 meters) of water on the front of French Reef.*

D. A diver explores Hourglass Cave on French Reef.

E. Bermuda chub, Kyphosus sectatrix, *swarm past a brain coral on French Reef.*

F. Common snook, Centropomus undecimalis, *are often seen on French Reef, and allow divers to get fairly close when approached slowly.*

G. This impressive photograph of glass minnows and a predatory snook was shot in a cave at French Reef.

H. This green moray eel, Gymnothorax funebris, *can be observed under one of the many coral ledges at French Reef.*

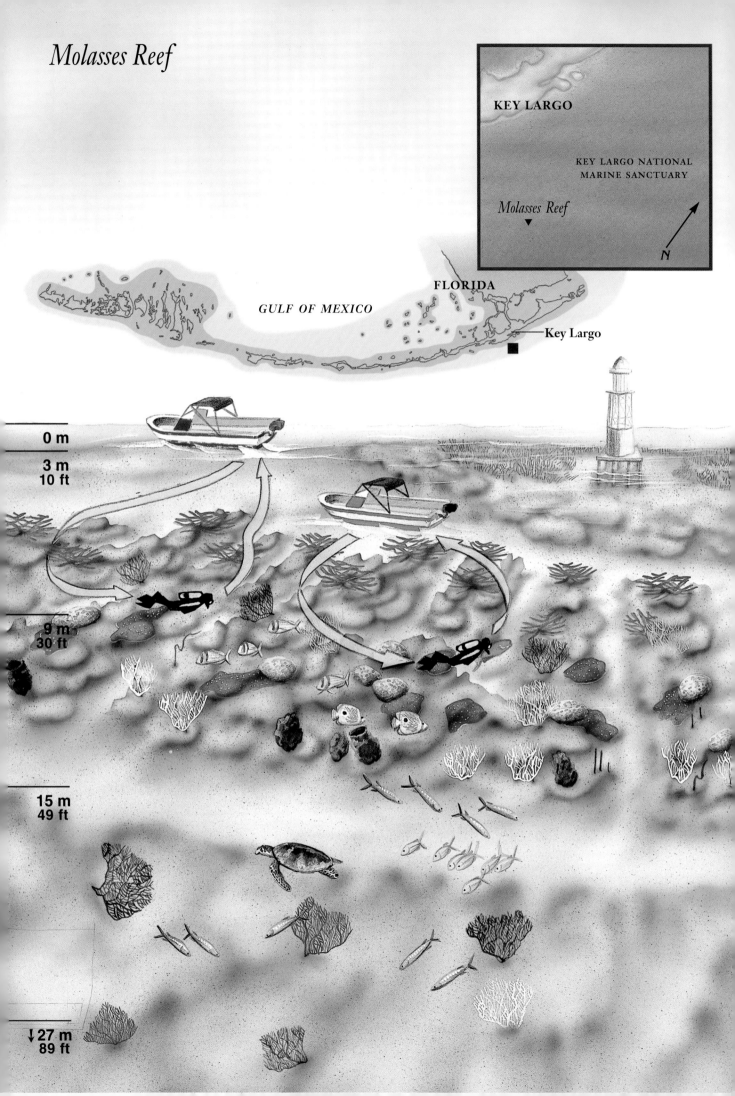

Molasses Reef

KEY LARGO

KEY LARGO NATIONAL
MARINE SANCTUARY

Molasses Reef
▼

N

FLORIDA

GULF OF MEXICO

Key Largo

0 m
3 m
10 ft

9 m
30 ft

15 m
49 ft

↓27 m
89 ft

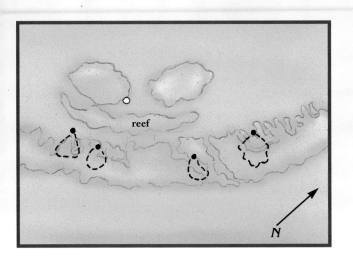

reef

N

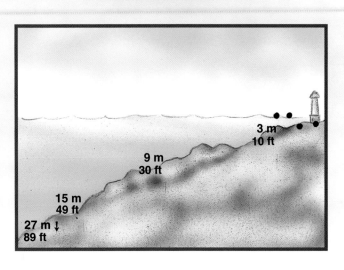

3 m
10 ft

9 m
30 ft

15 m
49 ft

27 m
89 ft

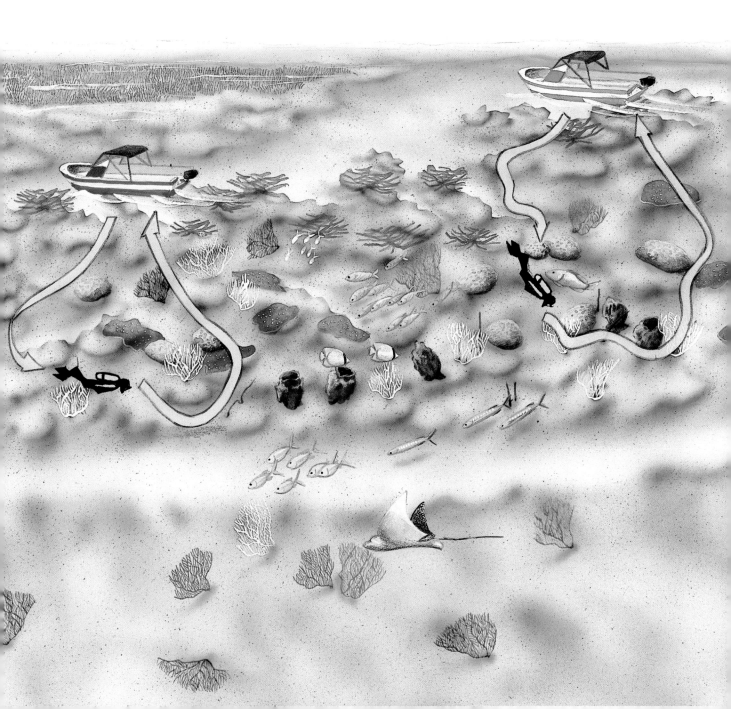

M olasses Reef is a perennial favorite for divers in the Florida Keys and may be the most popular dive site in the world. As many as 250,000 divers and snorkelers visit Molasses each year, drawn by its consistently good visibility, extensive coral coverage, and prolific fish life. It is also conveniently located straight out from one of the largest commercial marinas in the Florida Keys, home to many dive and snorkel boats.

Molasses Reef is named for the barge that grounded there many years ago while carrying a load of molasses barrels. Ship groundings have been a part of the history of this lovely reef for hundreds of years. The worst may have been the grounding of the *M/V Wellwood*, a 400-foot (122-meter) freighter that was driven high onto the reef in 1984. The hull completely pulverized 3 very old star coral formations and bulldozed a large flat spot on the reef that is still visible. The sanctuary has undertaken a restoration program to assist in the recovery of the reef. In spite of this area of localized damage, Molasses is still at the top of many divers' lists.

It is a large reef with diving depths from about 10 to over 70 feet (3 to 21.3 meters). Thirty-three mooring buoys mark sites on the reef, such as the Spanish Anchor, the Winch Hole, Fire Coral Caves, Hole in the Wall, and many others. The mooring buoys closest to the navigation light mark the shallowest dive sites, and each successive line of buoys gets deeper.

There are 3 distinct habitats on the reef, starting at the spur-and-groove formation that runs from the shallowest part of the living coral to about 30 feet (9 meters). The spurs are covered with hard and soft corals and rise 10 to 15 feet (3 to 4.6 meters) off the bottom. There is a small ledge at about 30 feet (9 meters) that marks the transition to the middle reef. The coral becomes less vertical and the ratio of hard to soft coral begins to favor soft corals in this section. Small barrel sponges begin to dot the bottom and

A

C

B

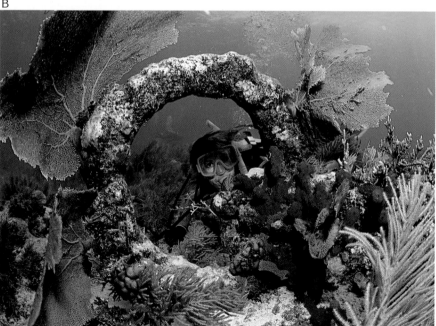

tube sponges appear more frequently. Larger barrel sponges and deep water sea fans dominate the bottom life, along with sporadic heads of giant star coral and mounds of star coral, at 45 or 50 feet (13.7 or 15.2 meters). This is the deep reef, which slopes until it reaches a lip at about 65 feet (19.8 meters). At this point the reef drops steeply to 70 or 75 feet (21.3 or 23 meters) and corals become very sparse on the sandy bottom.

Molasses Reef always seems to have a special gift for every diver, no matter how often they dive there. Divers routinely encounter green and hawksbill turtles, spotted eagle rays, green moray eels, and southern stingrays. There are always many schools of fish here, behaving naturally because they have not been fed by divers. If you are careful and patient, you can swim in the midst of closely packed schools of horse-eye jacks, permit jacks, bar jacks, yellow goatfish, small-mouth grunts, and great barracuda. Schools of 5 to 10 black-and-silver Atlantic spadefish tolerate a very close approach when you move slowly. Silvery snook are frequently seen on Molasses Reef, along with dark blue midnight parrotfish and lighter-colored blue parrotfish. Even bull sharks and great hammerheads have been seen from time to time.

The Molasses magic is just as strong once the sun goes down. Molasses Reef vignettes turn from daytime blue and green to brilliant red, orange, and purple when illuminated by divers' lights at night. The parrotfish rest in coral crevices, nestled in their protective mucus cocoons. The schools of snappers, jacks, and grunts have dispersed to feed and the nocturnal shift is emerging. Spiny lobsters walk out in the open and long-legged spider crabs feed on bits of algae. Octopuses make their fluid way across the reef on 8 sinuous tentacles, and millions of tiny coral polyps extend their own delicate tentacles to feed.

Molasses is located 5.5 nautical miles (10.1 kilometers) from the south portion of Key Largo. The reef crest is very shallow, but dive depths range from 10 to 90 feet (3 to 27.4 meters). Visibility is usually 40 to 80 feet (12.2 to 24.3 meters), with frequent periods of greater visibility when blue water is present. Like the Elbow, Molasses is exposed to the waves, which can occasionally be rough. Currents can vary from site to site on the reef at the same time of day. The strongest currents are generally felt on the south end of the reef.

Molasses Reef has been designated as one of the 18 Sanctuary Preservation Areas within the Florida Keys National Marine Sanctuary. Special care must be taken to avoid any damage to the coral. Fishing and lobstering are prohibited.

D

E

F

G

A. This aerial view of Molasses Reef shows dive boats tied to mooring buoys installed by the Key Largo National Marine Sanctuary. The spur-and-groove coral formations typical of Florida Keys outer bank reefs are clearly visible.

B. A diver observes the Spanish anchor that gives its name to the popular dive site at Molasses Reef.

C. The Winch Hole dive site on Molasses Reef. This ship's winch is thought to have belonged to the Slobodna, a 170-foot (52-meter) wooden schooner built in 1884 that ran aground on Molasses Reef in 1887.

D. The Spanish anchor at Molasses Reef is probably one of the anchors of the schooner Slobodna.

E. Creole wrasses, Clepticus parrae, wait patiently to be cleaned of parasites by a juvenile Spanish hog-fish, Bodianus rufus, on Molasses Reef.

F. A spotfin butterfly-fish, Chaetodon ocellatus, hovers near a large formation of pillar coral, Dendrogyra cylindrus, at the south end of Molasses Reef.

G. Molasses Reef has many coral arches like this one. Care should be taken when swimming through to avoid contact with the coral growing inside the arch.

Spiegel Grove

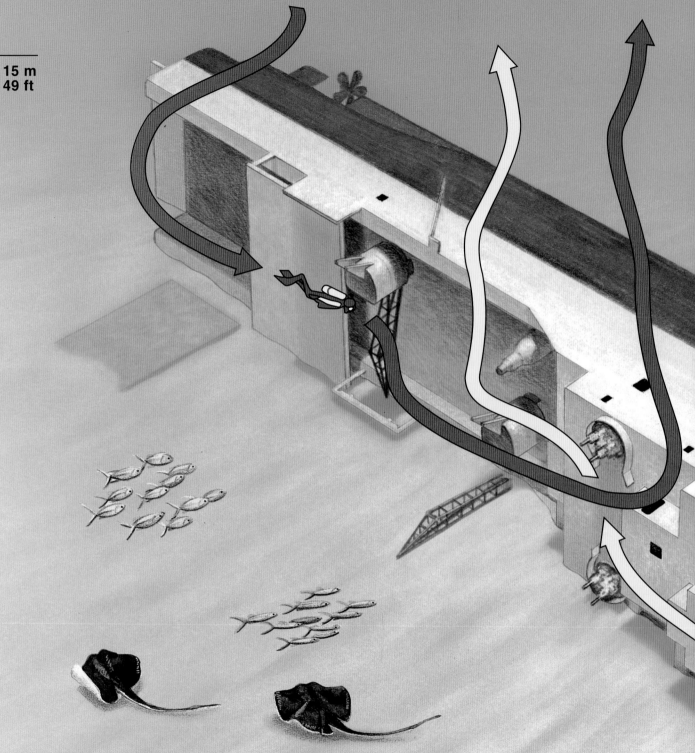

**15 m
49 ft**

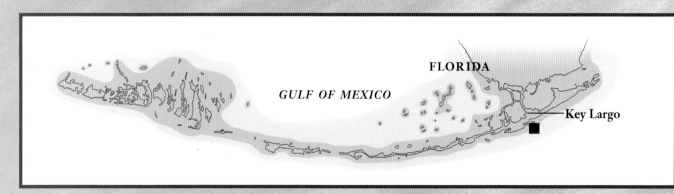

FLORIDA

GULF OF MEXICO

Key Largo

KEY LARGO

KEY LARGO NATIONAL
MARINE SANCTUARY

Spiegel Grove (LSD-32)

N

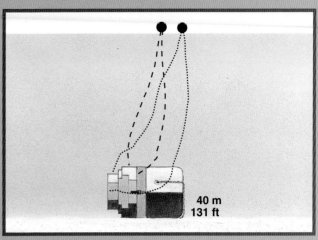

40 m
131 ft

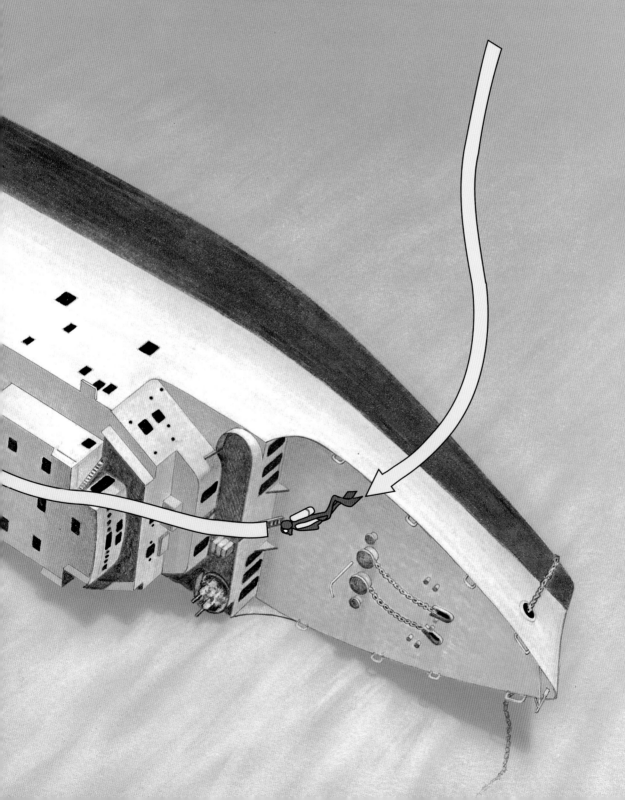

40 m
131 ft

The former USS *Spiegel Grove* is a behemoth among wrecks, the largest vessel ever made into an artificial reef for divers at the time of her sinking on June 17, 2002. An ex-naval amphibious assault ship designated LSD-32 (Landing Ship Dock), the *Spiegel Grove* is 510 feet (153 meters) long with a beam of 84 feet (25 m). Even resting on her starboard side in 125 feet (38 m) of water, the ship comes to within 50 feet (15 m) of the surface. The wreck is located about five miles (8 km) offshore from Key Largo, Florida, in the Florida Keys National Marine Sanctuary.

The *Spiegel Grove* was launched by the Ingalls Shipbuilding Corp. of Pascagoula, Mississippi, on November 10, 1955. The ship's unique design was built around her large well deck, where a variety of amphibious assault vehicles were carried. A complex system of internal tanks allowed up to 17 feet (5 m) of water to flood the well deck, creating a sea-going dock. The entire stern was opened and closed by a massive, hydraulic gate, which permitted up to 21 mechanized amphibious craft to drive in and out with ease. About a third of the well deck was spanned by an enormous helicopter deck, which held as many as eight helicopters, or was used as storage space for trucks. Two high capacity cranes allowed the *Spiegel Grove* to load and unload its cargo of vehicles without outside assistance. The long arm of the starboard crane broke free of its mount when the ship sank, and now extends out over the sand. The boarding ladder used to evacuate the ship when it sank prematurely is still attached to the hull next to the port crane.

The *Spiegel Grove* depended primarily on other warships and aircraft for protection, but three twin anti-aircraft guns provided a measure of defense. One gun mount is on the starboard side forward of the superstructure, and the other two are located on the port and starboard sides, aft of the superstructure. The barrels were cut off when the ship was decommissioned, but otherwise the gun mounts are largely intact and are easily recognized by their prominent recoil springs.

The uppermost deck of the ship is the 03 level. The wheelhouse is located here and a bronze plaque describing the ship's history

A

B

C

A. Spiegel Grove in Key Largo prior to sinking. A small army of volunteers worked for four days to complete the final clean-up and cut additional diver access holes to the main deck level (not shown in this photo).

B. After the stern flooded prematurely, the Spiegel Grove *turned over and floated with her bow high in the air. A marine salvage company put the ship down on her starboard side about two weeks later.*

C. A diver swims forward along a ladder leading down from the navigation bridge level.

D. One of three twin anti-aircraft gun mounts remaining on the Spiegel Grove. *The long barrels were cut off by the Navy when the ship was decommissioned, but the rest of the mechanisms are intact.*

E. The bow of the Spiegel Grove, *now about 95 feet (27 m) deep.*

F. One of the Spiegel Grove's *large bronze propellers. Both props and rudders are still in place.*

G. The foredeck of the Spiegel Grove, *showing the ship's massive anchor chains and anchor windlasses.*

can be found on the aft bulkhead, at about 95 feet (29 m). In the Command Information Center, directly behind the wheelhouse, several radars are still mounted, along with an old analog tracking table. The captain's day cabin was located on the starboard side, and various offices occupied the remainder of the deck.

The next deck down, the 02 level, is nearly twice as large as the navigation deck and contains the officers' wardroom and staterooms.

The 01 level is the largest of the upper decks. In addition to berthing spaces for the

ship's crew, this deck is where the mess hall and galley were located. The "Spiegel Beagle," a cartoon Snoopy riding an alligator, can be found on this deck in the athwartships (i.e., side to side) passageway on this level at a depth of about 95 feet (29 m).

The main deck, or 00 level, is partially split by the forward end of the well deck. Exiting the superstructure at the forward end of this level leads you out to the foredeck, where the anchor windlasses are located. Toward the stern, this level exits to the main deck along the top of the well deck wing walls. Berthing space for the ship's complement of 300 marines are found on this deck.

Most points of interest are on the super-structure side of the ship, but several features make visiting the hull side on at least one dive worthwhile. The two huge five-bladed propellers are here, along with the shafts and rudders. Driven by two steam turbines putting out a total of 24,000 shaft horse-power, her propellers cruised the *Spiegel Grove* at 22 knots. If you want a photo of yourself with the ship's name in the background, you can find it in two places at the stern. One is on the side of the hull, the other is on the back of the stern gate.

The *Spiegel Grove* was named after the Fremont, Ohio estate of President Rutherford B. Hayes. During her commissioned service from 1955 to 1989, the ship conducted two humanitarian tours to Africa,

distributing food, clothing and medicine, and served with the 6th Fleet off the east coast of the United States and in the Mediterranean. In addition to the removal of contaminants and general clean-up performed prior to sinking the ship, several provisions were made to improve diver access and safety.

First, all the doors above the main deck were either removed or secured in the open position. Second, four foot (1.2 m) by four foot holes were systematically cut in the bulkheads and decks above the main deck to provide *up or out* escape routes. Third, a series of guide lines were installed on each deck above the main deck. Except for the line running through the galley on deck 01, all of the guide lines begin and end at openings to the ocean. A system of red and green

D

E

F

G

mesh markers was also installed on each line. Going in the direction of the green mesh provides the shortest way out, although this may not necessarily be the shallowest route. Six moorings were installed after the ship sank, arranged along the port side from bow to stern. Use of the moorings is free, but due to high demand the normal etiquette is to vacate your mooring after one dive rather than sit on it during your surface interval. Dive conditions can be highly variable at the site, and a substantial current is often present. Depending on wind strength and direction, wave action may also be high. Visibility averages around 50 feet (15 m), but can be anywhere from 20 to 120 feet (6 to 36 m).

The Duane

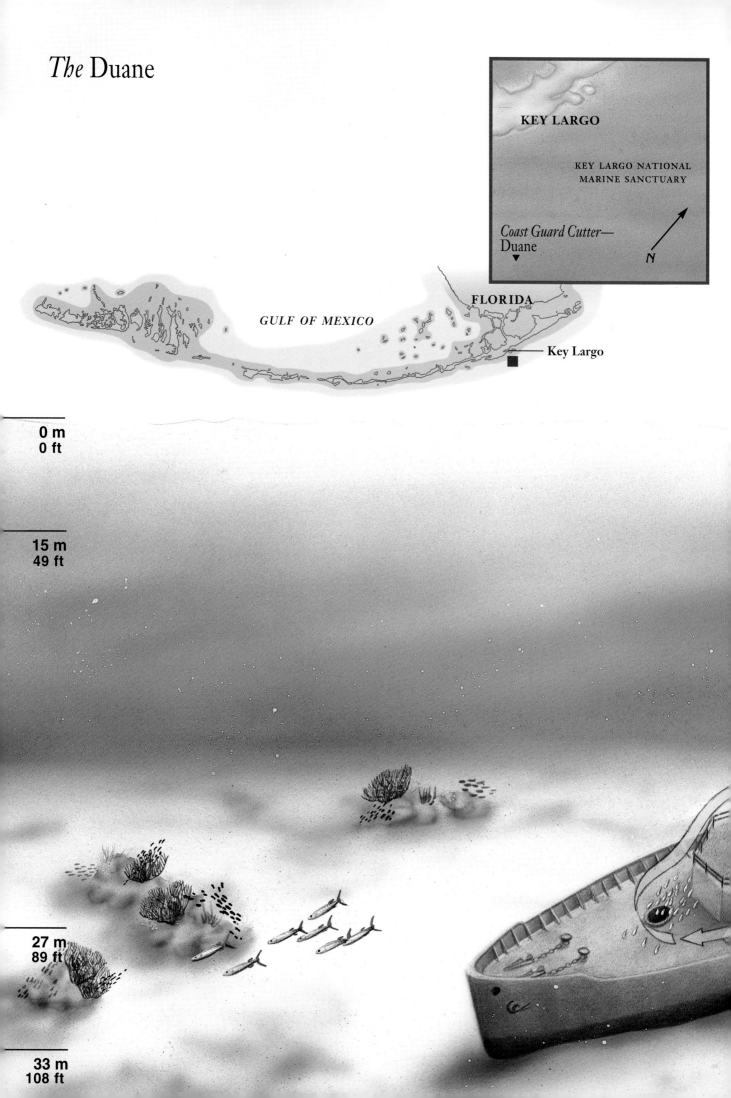

KEY LARGO

KEY LARGO NATIONAL
MARINE SANCTUARY

Coast Guard Cutter—
Duane
▼

N

FLORIDA

GULF OF MEXICO

Key Largo

0 m
0 ft

15 m
49 ft

27 m
89 ft

33 m
108 ft

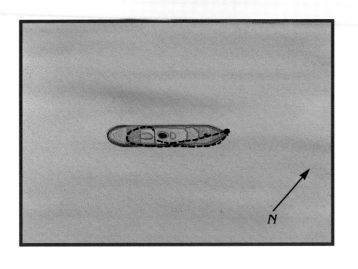

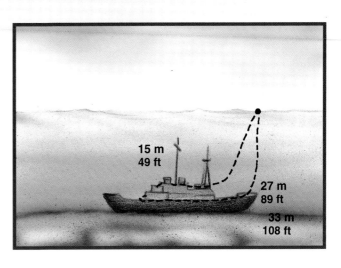

A

Named in honor of former secretary of the Treasury William J. Duane, this U.S. Coast Guard Cutter was built in 1935. Powered by twin Westinghouse steam turbines, the *Duane* was 327 feet (99.7 meters) long with a 41-foot (12.5-meter) beam. The *Duane* rests upright in about 120 feet (36.6 meters) of water. Due to the depth of water and frequent presence of strong currents, this wreck is suited only to experienced divers. It was carefully prepared for diving safety by re-

A. The Duane *on site off Key Largo, 1987. This 327-foot (100-meter) Coast Guard cutter had been meticulously cleaned prior to the sinking.*

B. The Duane *was a ghostly sight, sitting upright on the bottom, the day after the sinking in 1987.*

B

D

C

E

moving doors above the main deck and sealing access to the lower compartments. However, divers have reopened some entryways in order to penetrate more of the ship's interior passages. Penetrations of any kind should only be made by divers with the proper training, equipment, and experience. In 1980, the *Duane* actually sailed these waters on the way to Key West for escort duty during the massive Mariel boat lift, which brought thousands of refugees to the Florida Keys from Cuba. That action was very near the end of an illustrious career that included

C. The tripod legs and steel crow's nest of the Duane's *aft mast attract hundreds of fish, including barracuda, permit, jacks, and snappers.*

D. A diver using a propulsion vehicle descends toward the main deck of the Duane *through a cloud of fish.*

F

G

The *Duane* is located about 6 nautical miles (11.1 kilometers) offshore, less than 1 mile from Molasses Reef. Depths on the *Duane* range from 40 to 110 feet (12.2 to 33.5 meters). Visibility is normally 40 to 100 feet (12.2 to 30.4 meters), but can be spectacular when the blue Gulf Stream water is over the wreck. Currents vary from day to day. It can be calm one day and running very strongly the next. In fact, the currents on this wreck can change substantially in the course of several hours.

G. Divers peer into the bridge of the Duane, *already encrusted with coral and sponge.*

H. A pair of divers prepares to enter the wheelhouse of the Duane.

I. A great barracuda, Sphyraena barracuda, *is frequently found on the bridge of the* Duane.

H

E. A diver discovers a trumpetfish, Aulostomus maculatus, *on the starboard side of the* Duane's *main deck.*

F. The sun rays filtering through the water dramatically illuminate the tripod legs and crow's nest of the Duane.

sinking a U-boat with sister ship *Spencer* in 1941. The *Duane* later had the honor of acting as the flagship of General John O'Daniel, head of Operation Dragoon during the invasion of France. During the Vietnam conflict, the *Duane* patrolled the coast of Vietnam as part of the Coastal Surveillance Force. During her 50-year career, however, the *Duane*'s most important accomplishment is the number of lives saved during rescue operations. In the course of war and peace the men and women serving aboard this noble vessel risked their lives to save others.

I

Pickles Reef

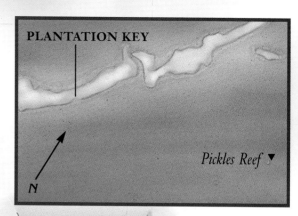

PLANTATION KEY

Pickles Reef ▼

N

FLORIDA

GULF OF MEXICO

■ Plantation Key

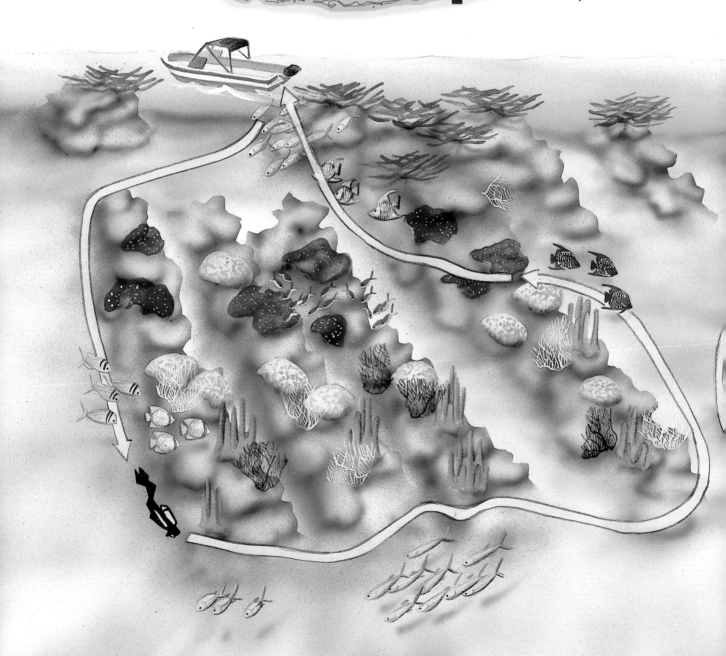

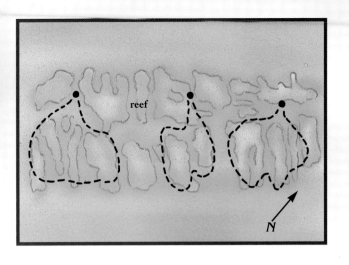

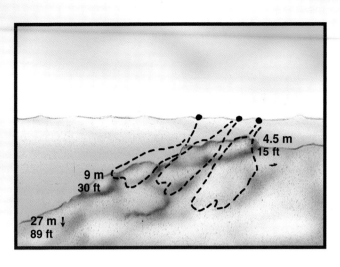

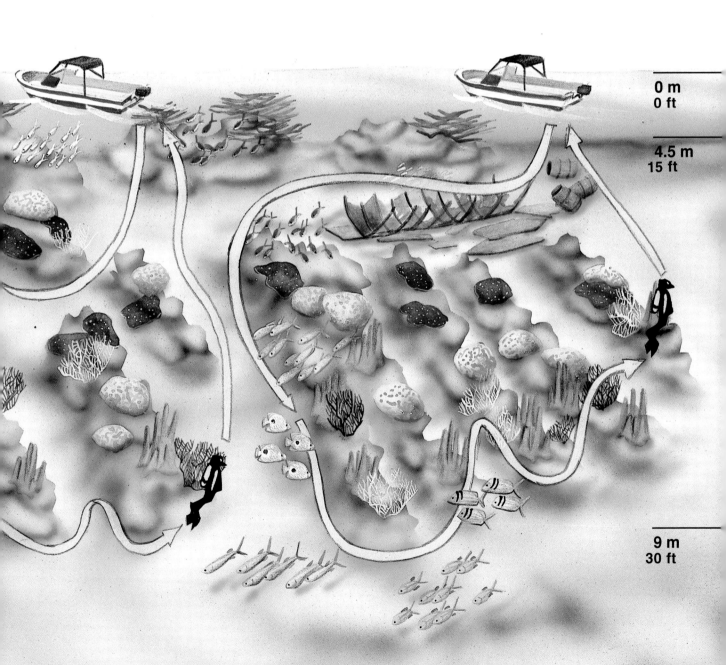

Pickles Reef is the next major reef south of Molasses Reef. It is not marked by navigation aids and less visited by divers, so fish life thrives. Its name derives from kegs, thought to be pickle barrels, found on the reef. It is more likely that the kegs contained mortar to be used in construction in the Lower Keys. The diving depths here range from 15 to about 30 feet (4.6 meters to 9 meters). The reef tends to get very sparse in deeper waters. In the shallows, however, it is a virtual aquarium.

Bring along a waterproof fish or coral guide and just swim along leisurely, enjoying and identifying the sea life, and you will have a great dive. An

A. Bluestriped grunts, Haemulon sciurus, and French grunts, Haemulon flavolineatum, look for shelter among the spires of a colony of pillar coral. Pillar coral is one of the few hard corals that regularly extends its tentacles to feed during the day.

B. Thanks to the clear water and the plentiful reef fish, this area is a favorite for Keys divers.

C. Bluestriped grunts, French grunts, and yellow goatfish, Mulloidichthys martinicus, school close to Pickles Reef.

D. A trumpetfish, Aulostomus maculatus, hovers next to a sea plume, Pseudopterogorgia, to conceal itself from both predators and potential prey.

E. Grunts school near an arch marked by a large orange elephant ear sponge, Agelas clathrodes.

observant diver can easily find 25 or more species of fish on one dive. A good way to see lots of fish is to settle down on the sand near a large coral head. Remain as motionless as possible, controlling hand and fin movements, and breathe with a moderate, even cadence. After 5 minutes or so, the fish will get used to your presence, come out of hiding, and swim without concern right before your eyes. Some of the more curious species, such as blue angelfish and Nassau groupers, may actually swim right up to your mask to peer at you. Another curious fish that frequents Pickles Reef is the tarpon. These large fish weigh as much as 80 or 90 pounds (36.3 or 41 kilograms) and are covered in mirrorlike scales. They tend to hang about under ledges or cruise the reef in small groups.

One of the largest pillar coral colonies in the Florida Keys, Pillar Coral Forest, lies at the north end of the reef. Even though pillar coral is relatively fast growing, it is not widely distributed along the reefs. Its tall, thin spires distinguish it distinctly from other corals. Pillar coral also commonly feeds during the day, unlike most other hard corals. The polyps are not round and the tentacles are so closely packed that it looks like furry brown tubes stacked upright and close together.

Pickles Reef is about 5.5 nautical miles (10.1 kilometers) off the southern portion of Key Largo. Depths range from 20 to 90 feet (6 to 27.4 meters). Visibility is usually 40 to 70 feet (12.2 to 21.3 meters). Currents are not usually strong but can vary from dive to dive.

F. This close-up photograph shows an orange ball corallimorph, Pseudocorynactis caribbeorum.

G. Bluestriped grunts and French grunts share the shelter of a ledge grown over with elkhorn coral, Acropora palmata, *to escape predators during the day.*

H. Yellow goatfish, Mulloidichthys martinicus, *huddle close in a school for mutual protection.*

I. Squirrelfish, Holocentrus adscensionis, *beneath a ledge on Pickles Reef.*

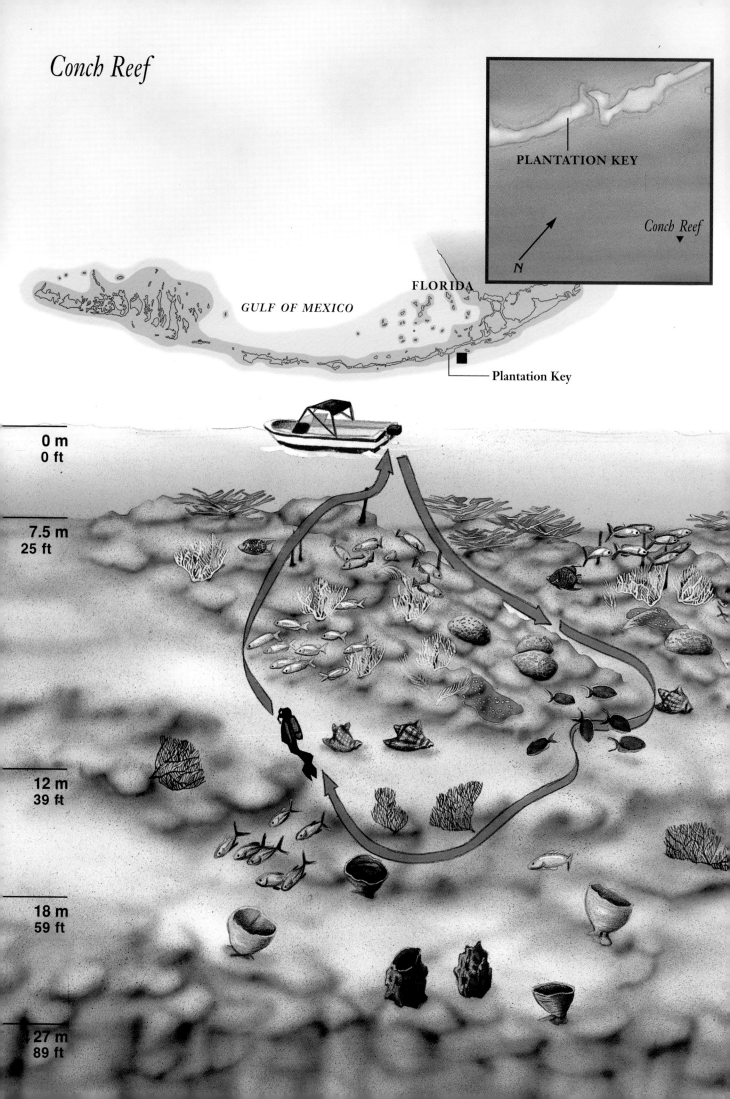

Conch Reef

GULF OF MEXICO

FLORIDA

PLANTATION KEY

Conch Reef

N

Plantation Key

0 m
0 ft

7.5 m
25 ft

12 m
39 ft

18 m
59 ft

27 m
89 ft

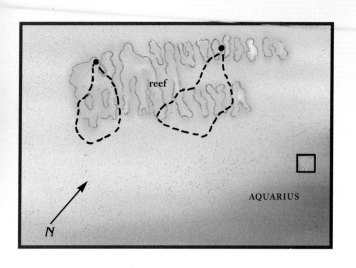

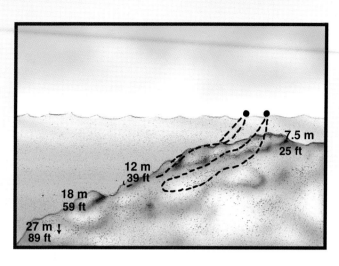

L arge numbers of queen conch live in the sand flats and sea grass on the back side of Conch Reef. You can see them easily, moving slowly along in about 10 or 20 feet (3 or 6 meters) of water. Longtime local residents, especially people actually born in the Keys and Key West, are sometimes referred to as "conchs." This nickname could have originated from the popularity of this marine snail as a food source in the Florida Keys or from the custom of placing a conch shell on a stick in front of a house in which a baby had been born.

In spite of the way it is spelled, conch is pronounced "konk." One sure way to brand yourself a tourist is to soften the

B

A

C

"ch" sound. You must sample this local delicacy in a restaurant, however, because all conch are protected by law.

In 1980 the Florida Keys pretended to secede from the United States, taking the name "Conch Republic," in protest against the inconvenient government roadblocks set up in response to the influx of refugees in the Mariel boat lift. The lighthearted plan was to surrender to the United States government and draw foreign aid forever more.

Conch Reef is somewhat deeper than other reefs in the Keys, with much of the best diving in the 40-to-60-foot (12.2-to-18.2-meter) range. There is a great proportion of sponge life at this depth, particularly of the impres-

sive giant barrel sponges. Hundreds of these large animals inhabit this reef, some as tall as 5 feet (1.5 meters). Like corals, these are slow-growing organisms and a large specimen can be up to 100 years old.

The reef drops off from 60 to about 90 feet (18.2 to 27.4 meters), flattening out from that point into a gradually sloping sand bottom. Known as Conch Wall, this is one of the few places in the Keys where the reef is prolific at this depth. Deepwater sea fans take advantage of the current that flows along the wall, reaching out with lacy fingers to filter the water. A powerful dive light or strobe reveals the maroon or even bright red colors of these soft corals.

The Aquarius Underwater Habitat is one of the unusual features of Conch Reef. This state-of-the-art research facility allows scientists to spend days or even weeks on the bottom, conducting research into the most pressing questions of coral reef ecology. Aquarius is operated by the National Undersea Research Center, which usually invites divers to come and take a look. Buoys are maintained in the vicinity of the habitat for divers' convenience. At times, however, the area is closed to prevent interruption of scientific experiments and to ensure the safety of the aquanauts during critical operations. Local dive operators are advised of the status of the habitat and information can be obtained from the Florida Keys National Marine Sanctuary.

Conch Reef is located about 5 nautical miles (9.3 kilometers) from the southern end of Key Largo. Depths range from 25 to 90 feet (7.6 to 27.4 meters). Visibility is usually 40 to 70 feet (12.2 to 21.3 meters). Currents are negligible to moderate, but strong currents are present occasionally.

The Florida Keys National Marine Sanctuary has established 2 areas of special protection on Conch Reef. The first is a Sanctuary Preservation Area that covers most of the main reef. Special protection is given to the corals here, so exercise an extra degree of caution with your buoyancy control

D

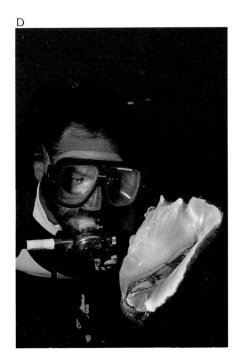

and fin placement. The fishing prohibition that usually accompanies a Sanctuary Preservation Area has been modified at Conch Reef to permit catch-and-release fishing. The second area of special protection is a Special Use Area set aside for research; you may enter only with a permit.

E

F

G

H

A. *Bluestriped grunts,* Haemulon sciurus, *French grunts,* Haemulon flavolineatum, *and schoolmasters,* Lutjanus apodus, *find protection near a sea fan on Conch Reef.*

B. *Divers should go to the Aquarius Underwater Habitat, where many scientists work on extended coral reef research projects.*

C. *Squirrelfish,* Holocentrus adscensionis, *are frequently seen throughout Conch Reef.*

D. *A diver observes a queen conch,* Strombus gigas, *a protected species in the Florida Keys.*

E. *Night dives are possible on Conch Reef. Many fish can be observed hunting, like this doctorfish,* Acanthurus bahianus.

F. *A spotted moray,* Gymnothorax moringa, *among rope sponges shows its frightening mouth to the photographer.*

G. *Smallmouth grunts,* Haemulon chrysargyreum, *can often be observed on the shallow coral fingers of Conch Reef.*

H. *A red shrimp stalks across encrusting sponges and coral in search of food at night on Conch Reef.*

Davis Reef

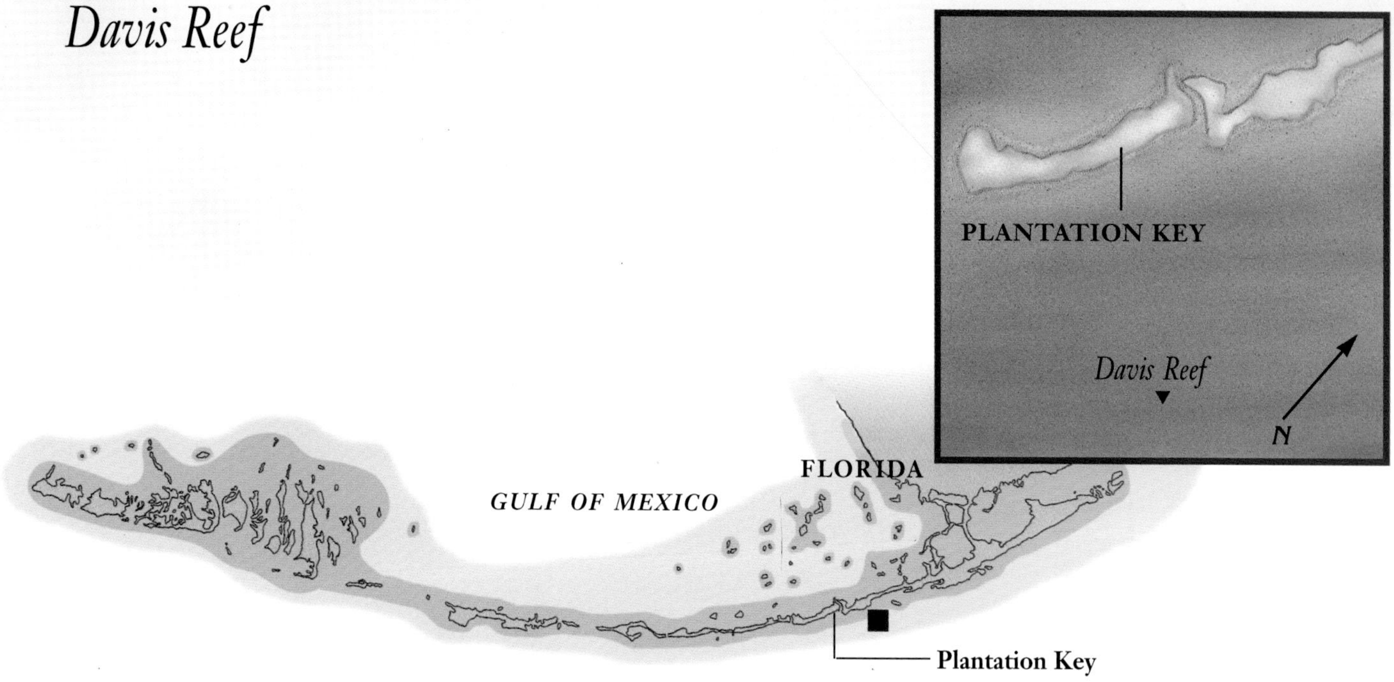

PLANTATION KEY

Davis Reef

N

GULF OF MEXICO

FLORIDA

Plantation Key

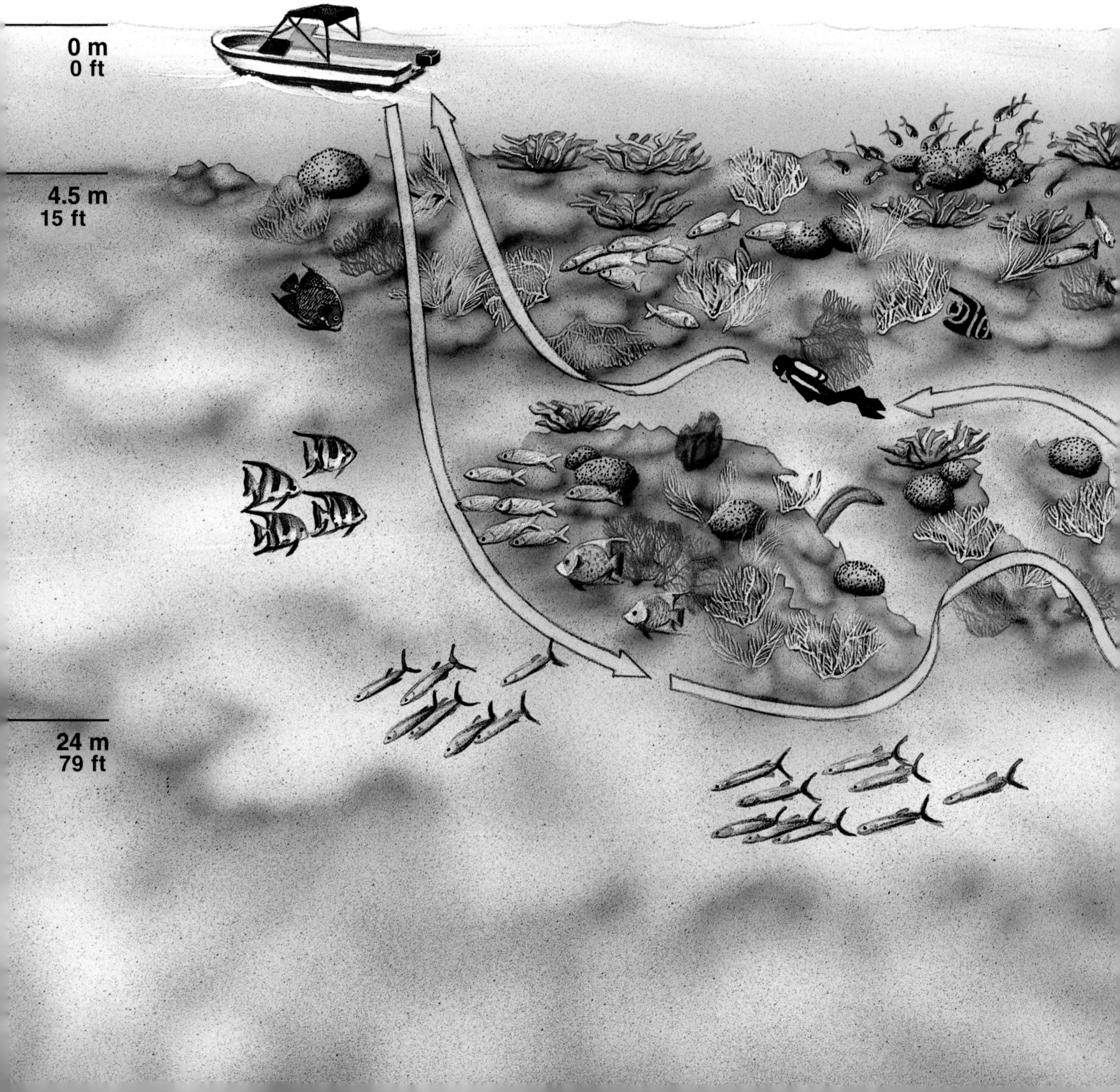

0 m
0 ft

4.5 m
15 ft

24 m
79 ft

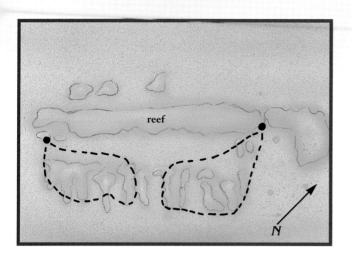

reef

N

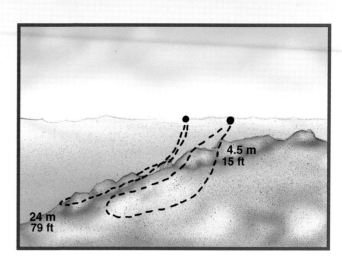

4.5 m
15 ft

24 m
79 ft

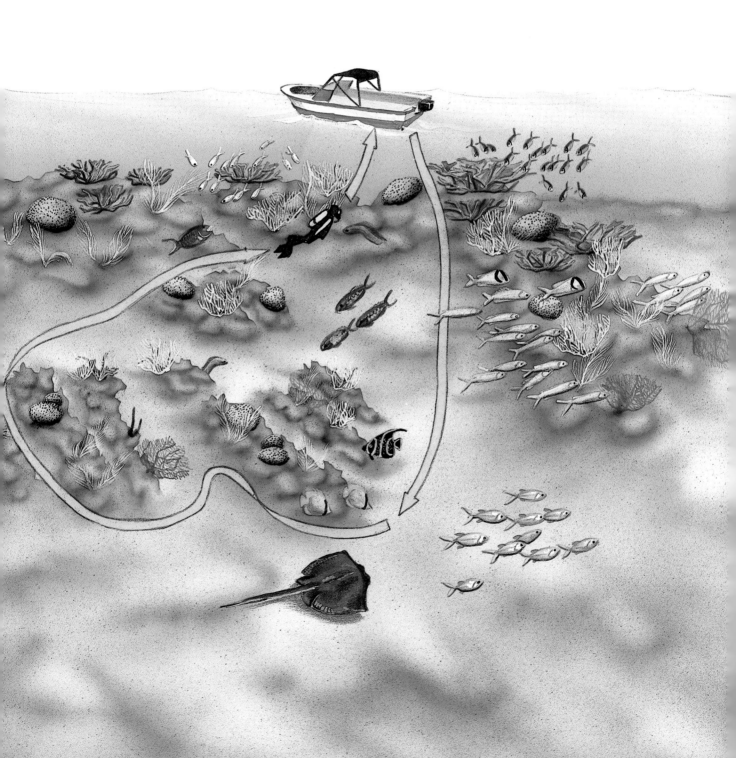

The main feature of Davis Reef is a 5-to-10-foot (1.5-to-3-meter) ledge that runs almost the entire length of the reef in about 30 feet (9 meters) of water. Dense schools of fish find refuge from predators in the shelter of this ledge. Groups of bluestriped grunts, cottonwicks, tomtate grunts, and Spanish grunts cluster together here like spectators in a stadium. Several different species often school together, so you may see yellow goatfish mixed with French grunts and porkfish with schoolmasters. To get the best

C

A

B

D

look at these schools, approach slowly until the fish start to move apart. Stop immediately and be as motionless as possible while breathing slowly and regularly. The fish will "polarize" again after a few minutes, lining up so that they are all facing in the same direction. At this point you can ease another foot or so closer.

Divers here often see the large and colorful rainbow parrotfish, one of the most impressive parrotfish in the terminal phase. Unusual groups of 4 and 5 of these fish can be spotted swimming together.

The crevices under the ledge provide habitats for many fish and invertebrates. You are almost certain to see green moray eels. Quite often an enormous eel will be found under the ledge. These eels are not usually aggressive: the opening and closing of their jaws, a motion that looks ominous and threatening, is actually a method of passing water over the gills for respiration. Nurse sharks are frequently seen here, either hunting under the ledges for the lobsters, octopuses, and small fish (their

A. Bluestriped grunts, Haemulon sciurus, *and French grunts,* Haemulon flavolineatum, *share the shelter of the Davis Reef ledge.*

B. The sun rays penetrate the surface and illuminate a huge school of bluestriped grunts, French grunts, and white grunts, Haemulon plumieri.

C. Caesar grunts, Haemulon carbonarium, *and bluestriped grunts swim in a densely packed school on Davis Reef.*

D. Davis Reef is known for its large numbers of green moray eels, Gymnothorax funebris.

E. A nurse shark,
Ginglymostoma
cirratum, *rests*
beneath the shallow
ledge at Davis Reef.

F. Spotted drums,
Equetus punctatus,
like this one on Davis
Reef, can be found on
many of the Florida
Keys outer bank reefs.
They tend to stay very
close to their holes in
the reef, diving out
of sight quickly, but
curiosity will bring
them back if you
are patient.

G. A stoplight parrot-
fish, Sparisoma
viride, *at night*
wedged safely in a
coral crevice.

H. Scrawled filefish,
Aluterus scriptus,
frequently seen
between 20 and 50
feet (6 and 15 meters)
on the outer reefs.

I. Giant star coral,
Montastrea
cavernosa, *feeding*
at night. When the
polyps are extended
like this, corals are
very easily damaged
by contact with divers'
fins, knees, or tanks.

E

F

G

H

favorite food) or resting in a protected spot. Nurse sharks are also not aggressive; in fact, their docile nature has made them an easy target for diver harassment. Many divers have been surprised by how fast a harassed nurse shark can turn and bite.

Photographers with a normal lens, close-up kit, or macrophotography setup are able to find many good subjects along the ledge. The elusive spotted drum can sometimes be coaxed out for photographs, along with spotted morays, butter hamlets, rock beauties, and spotfin butterflyfish.

Davis Reef is located 4.5 nautical miles (8.3 kilometers) off Plantation Key. Depths range from 15 to 80 feet

I

(4.6 to 24.3 meters). Visibility is usually 30 to 60 feet (9 to 18.2 meters). Currents vary from none to moderate. Davis Reef has been designated as a Sanctuary Preservation Area by the Florida Keys National Marine Sanctuary. Special care must be taken to avoid any damage to the coral, especially by misplaced anchors or careless buoyancy control.

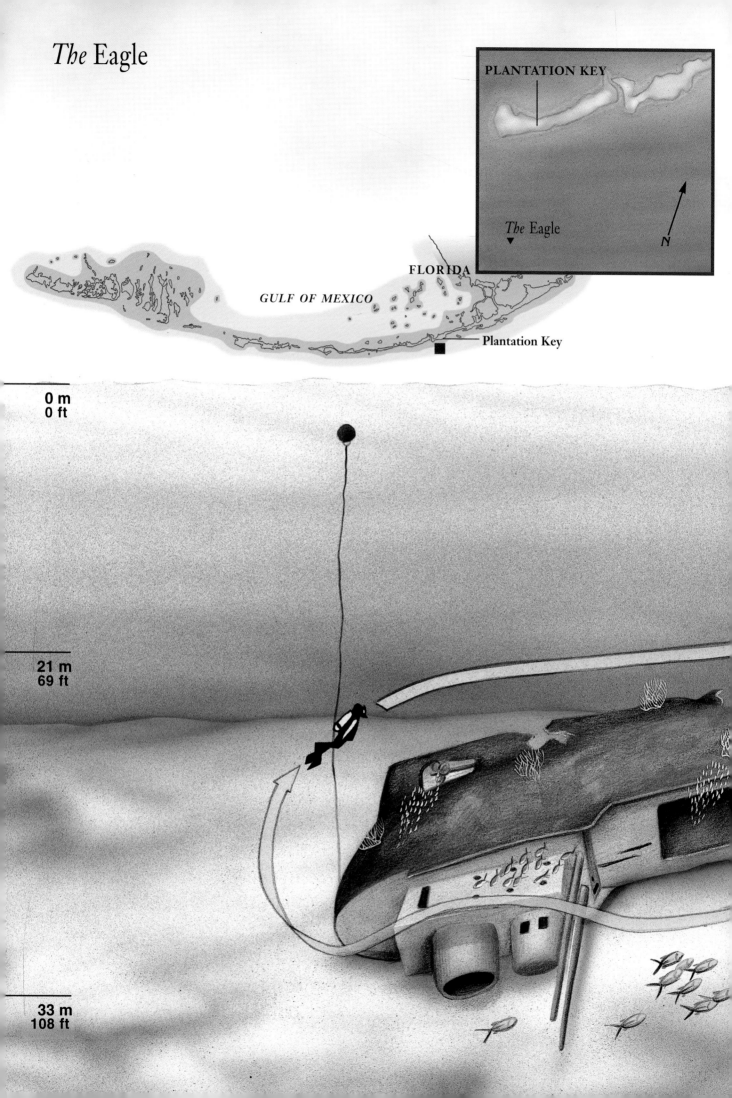

The Eagle

PLANTATION KEY

The Eagle

N

FLORIDA

GULF OF MEXICO

Plantation Key

0 m
0 ft

21 m
69 ft

33 m
108 ft

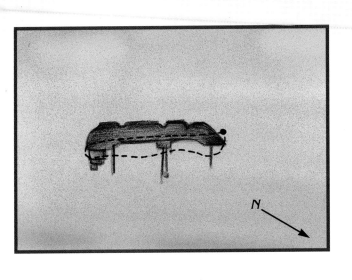

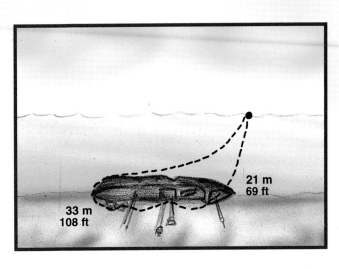

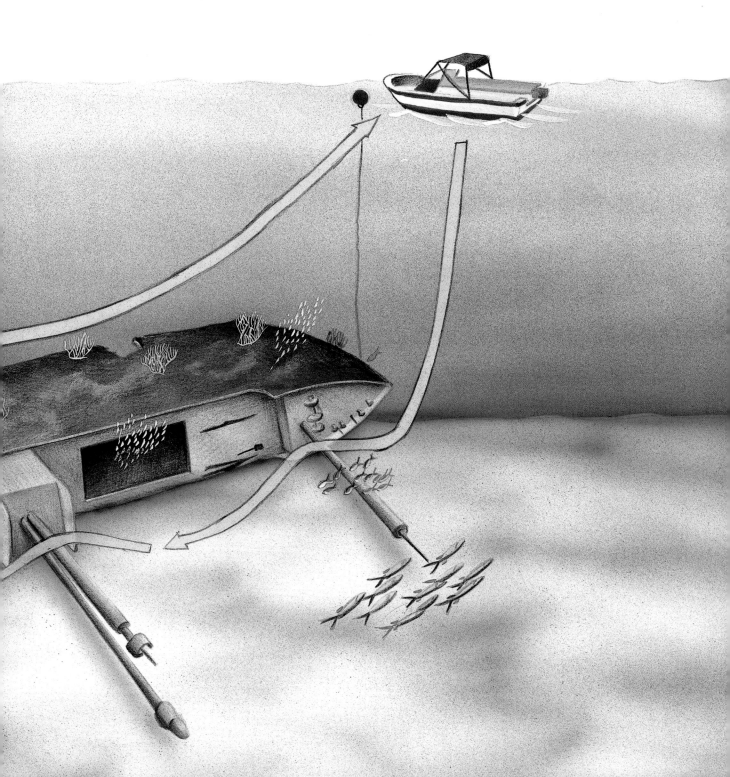

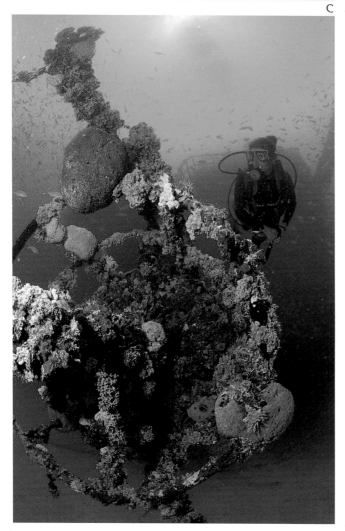

Originally named *Raila Dan*, this vessel was later named *Barok*, *Carmela*, *Ytai Carigulf Pioneer*, *Aaron K.*, and, finally, *Eagle*. She lies on her starboard side in 110 feet (33.5 meters) of water off the coast of Islamorada, sunk there on December 19, 1985, by members of the Islamorada community and the Eagle Tire Company. The *Eagle* was rapidly overgrown with encrusting corals and sponges and has become home to thousands of reef fish.

Constructed in Holland in 1962, the *Eagle* was 269 feet (82 meters) long with a beam of 40 feet (12.2 meters). Powered by a 10-cylinder diesel engine, she was capable of cruising at 12 knots. During

A. The Eagle, *a 269-foot (82-meter) freighter, just prior to her sinking on December 19, 1985.*

B. The exact moment of the explosion to sink the Eagle.

C. The crow's nest on the aft mast of the Eagle *is liberally coated with coral and sponge growth after a decade on the bottom.*

D. This panoramic photograph shows the superstructure of the Eagle, *which rests on her starboard side in about 110 feet (33.5 meters) of water.*

the latter portion of her life, operating as the *Aaron K.*, the ship was used to transport paper and cardboard from the United States to Central and South America. In 1985 fire broke out in the machinery spaces en route from Miami to Venezuela, damaging the vessel beyond repair. After being towed back to Miami, the *Aaron K.* was cleaned and prepped for diver safety and sent on one final voyage to the waters off Islamorada. Explosives planted by the Metro-Dade Bomb Squad were used to sink the vessel. Simultaneously, a series of harmless but spectacular charges were set off along the superstructure to add to the excitement of the event. Unfortunately, there was a problem with the way the ship was ballasted and she settled onto her starboard side, covering up large holes that had been carefully cut for diver entry and exit. The combination of open hatches and explosion holes leaves numerous entry points for properly trained and equipped divers. Inexperienced divers should attempt entry only with a guide.

The exterior of the ship has many areas of interest, including the completely encrusted crow's nest on the aft mast. The crow's nest sticks straight out from the ship at around 95 feet (29 meters) and is surrounded by large schools of fish. The large prop and rudder, also well covered with coral and sponges, rest at about the same

depth on the opposite side. There is a large open hatch that runs the entire width of the ship forward of the crow's nest. The main mast and a smaller forward mast jut out into the open water, like the crow's nest, attracting clouds of fish.

The *Eagle* is located about 5 nautical miles (9.3 kilometers) off Islamorada. Diving depths range from 70 to 110 feet (21.3 to 33.5 meters). Visibility is usually 40 to 70 feet (12.2 to 21.3 meters), frequently greater when the position of the Gulf Stream is favorable. As on the *Bibb* and *Duane*, currents change from day to day. Sometimes there may be little or no current and sometimes it may be very strong. These currents

are generated by the Gulf Stream or eddies from the Gulf Stream, rather than by tides, so there is no way to predict them.

E. The crow's nest on the aft mast of the Eagle, *photographed about a year after the sinking in 1985.*

F. The massive propeller and the rudder of the Eagle *have been heavily encrusted with sponge and coral.*

G. Large numbers of fish are attracted to the submerged superstructure of the Eagle.

H. Large, silver-scaled tarpon, Megalops atlanticus, are frequently seen on the wreck of the Eagle.

Coffins Patch

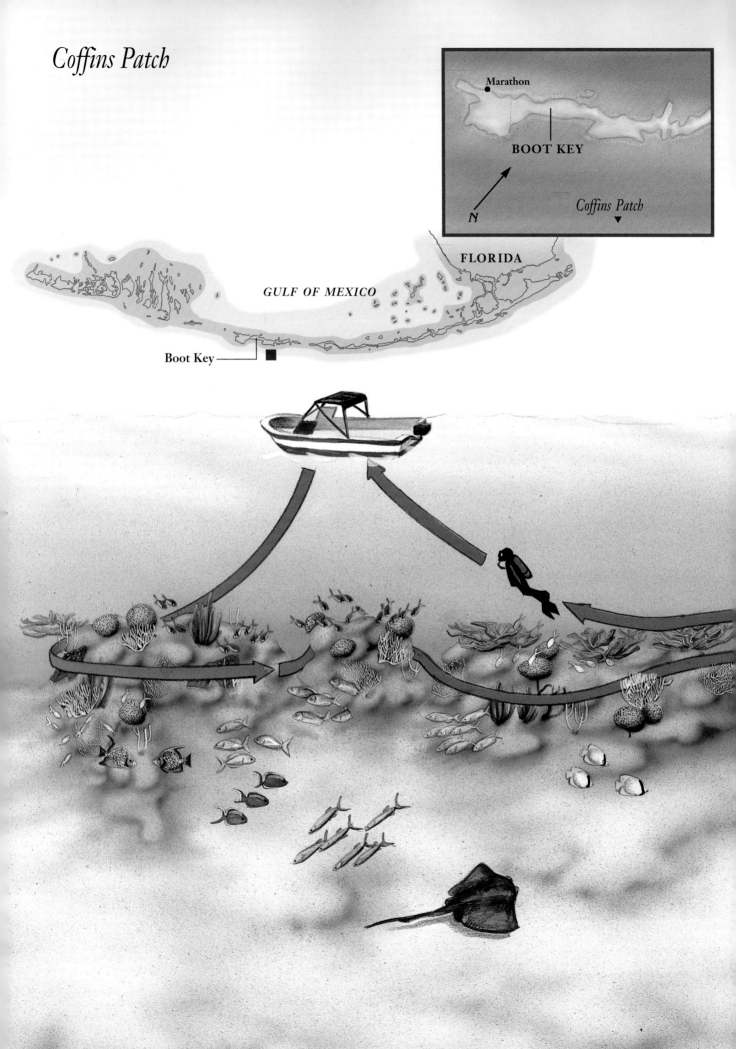

Marathon

BOOT KEY

N

Coffins Patch

FLORIDA

GULF OF MEXICO

Boot Key

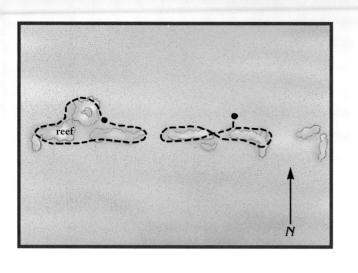

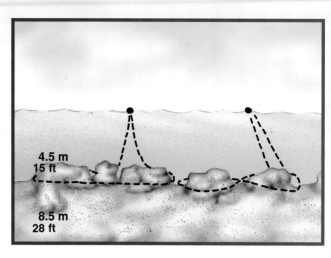

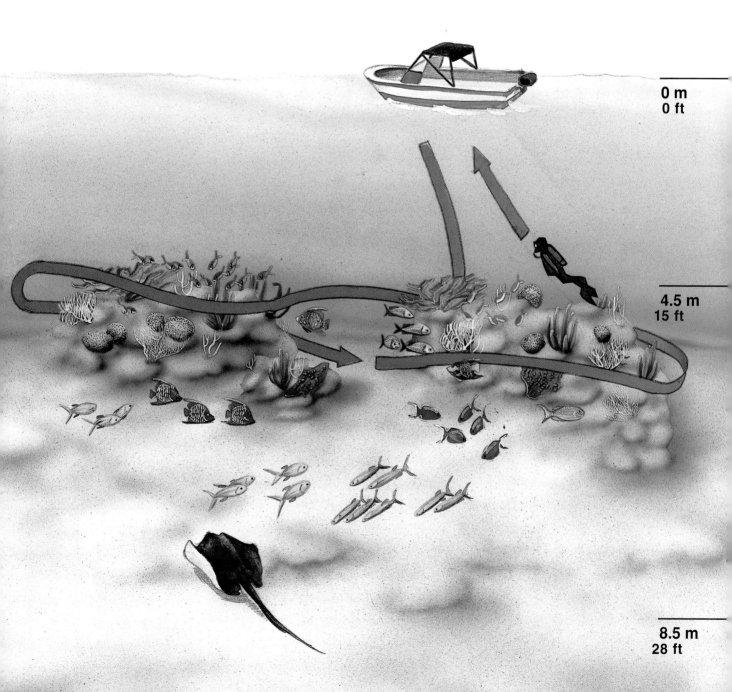

4.5 m
15 ft

8.5 m
28 ft

reef

N

0 m
0 ft

4.5 m
15 ft

8.5 m
28 ft

A. A spotted spiny lobster, Panulirus guttatus, *occupies an unusual hole in a colony of pillar coral,* Dendrogyra cylindrus, *on Coffins Patch.*

Coffins Patch covers a large area made up of half a dozen shallow reefs not far from the *Thunderbolt.* It is a favorite site for a second dive following a visit to the *Thunderbolt* because it lies at depths ranging from 15 to 30 feet (4.6 to 9 meters). These reefs exhibit the characteristics of patch reefs rather than bank reefs, with coral buildups around the complete circumference and shallow crests of live coral rather than rubble. There is a nice diversity of coral species, including many smooth brain corals the size of soccer balls, spheres of green convoluted brain coral, and globes of starlet coral. Pillar coral colonies have been growing steadily over the past 2 or 3 decades in several locations at Coffins Patch. They have expanded significantly the area they cover and are among the healthiest specimens in the Florida Keys.

A dive on the Coffins Patch is like swimming through a life-sized aquarium. Bring along a Caribbean fish guide book and you are likely to come across almost any of the fish in it. Four differ-

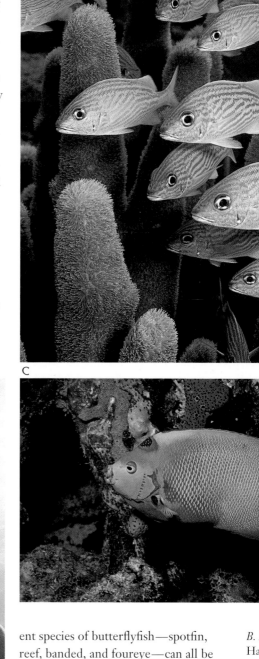

B

A

ent species of butterflyfish—spotfin, reef, banded, and foureye—can all be seen here. All 5 of the Florida Keys angelfish species, including queen, blue, French, gray, and rock beauty, are here, too, along with their distinctive juvenile forms. Grunts, parrotfish, and snappers swarm over the coral in great profusion, making Coffins Patch a delight for both snorkelers and divers.

Coffins Patch is located about 4 nautical miles (7.4 kilometers) offshore from Marathon. Depths range from 15 to 28 feet (4.6 to 8.5 meters).

B. French grunts, Haemulon flavolineatum, *seek shelter in the spires of pillar coral on Coffins Patch.*

C. Queen angelfish, Holacanthus ciliaris, *one of the most colorful angelfish, is found on many Florida Keys reefs, where it dines frequently on sponges.*

Visibility is usually from 25 to 50 feet (7.6 to 15.2 meters). Currents range from negligible to light.

Coffins Patch has been designated a Sanctuary Preservation Area to provide an extra measure of protection against damage to coral by divers and boaters. Avoid any contact with coral while diving and check to make sure your anchor is not touching any coral.

D. A trumpetfish, Aulostomus maculatus, *attempts to camouflage itself next to a Venus sea fan,* Gorgonia flabellum.

E. *These Christmas tree worms,* Spirobranchus giganteus, *are growing in a coral head. These colorful worms can be found at nearly any depth and on all reefs in the Florida Keys.*

F. *This spotted goatfish,* Pseudopeneus maculatus, *in its nighttime coloring, is resting on the sand.*

G. *This spiny lobster,* Panulirus argus, *was photographed at night on Coffins Patch. Since Coffins Patch is a Sanctuary Preservation Area, lobstering is not allowed.*

The Thunderbolt

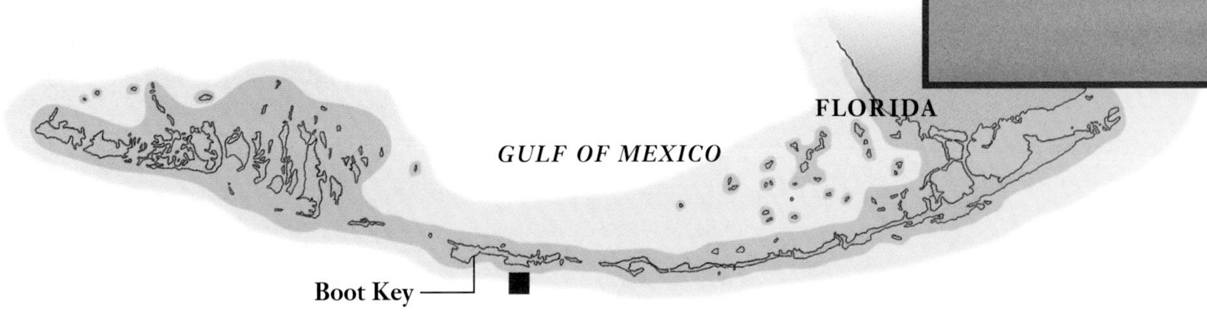

Marathon

BOOT KEY

The Thunderbolt

N

FLORIDA

GULF OF MEXICO

Boot Key

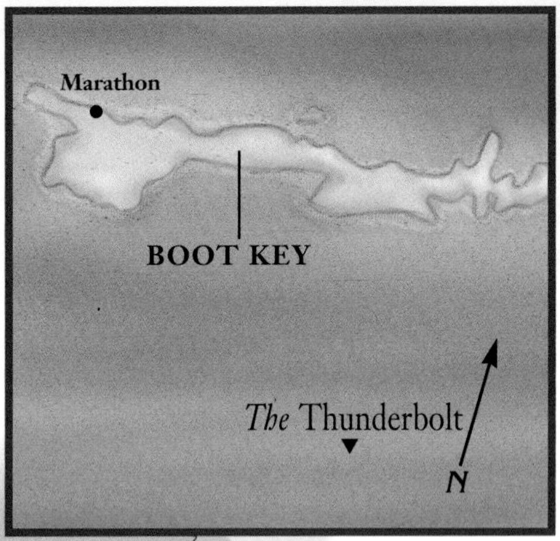

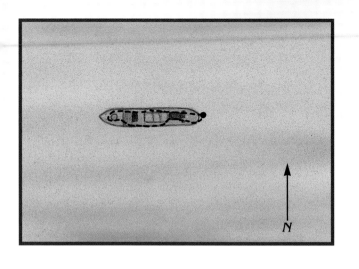

N

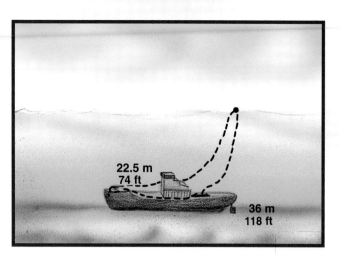

22.5 m
74 ft

36 m
118 ft

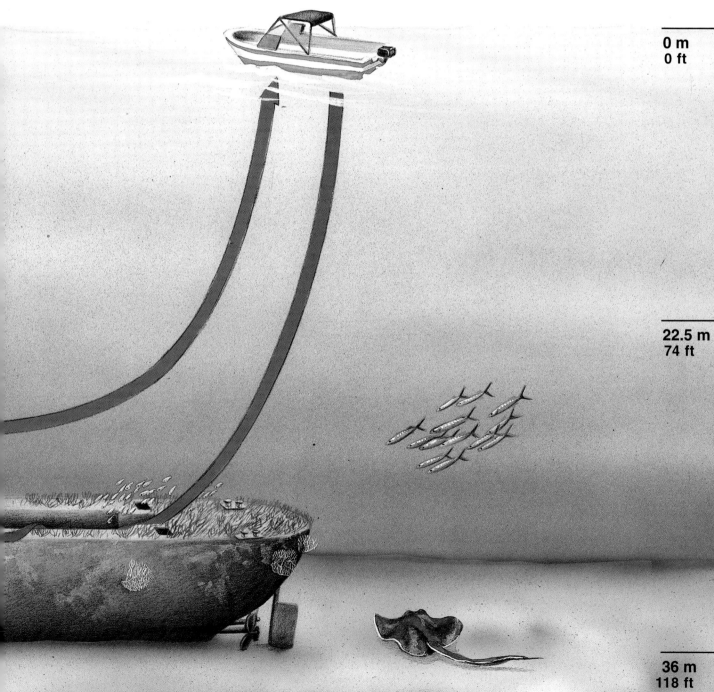

0 m
0 ft

22.5 m
74 ft

36 m
118 ft

One of the tasks of this vessel before it was sunk as an artificial reef was to collect information on lightning strikes. The Florida Power and Light Company mounted 2 jet engines on the ship, which were used to blow ionized particles into the atmosphere through a big stack. The particles attracted lightning to the ship, where the strikes were analyzed for research. The *Thunderbolt* derived her name from this hazardous duty.

Welded letters on the stern of the ship reveal her original name to be the *U.S.S. Randolph*, which was built in 1942 for the United States Army. The vessel was 188 feet (57.3 meters) long and outfitted to lay cable. She laid

A

B

C

D

many thousands of miles of cable before being sold to the power company and renamed *Thunderbolt*.

The vessel was sold for use in underwater surveying after the lightning research was finished. However, she sank at the dock on the Miami River before that service began. The local community in Marathon collected money to have her cleaned and towed to the Florida Keys. No explosives were used in the sinking to avoid creating dangerous jagged edges.

The *Thunderbolt* was scuttled quietly on March 3, 1986.

The vessel now rests upright in 120 feet (36.5 meters) of water. The bridge lies at about 80 feet (24.3 meters) and the top of the cable wheel is at about 85 feet (26 meters). The huge, open-spoked cable wheel still dominates the forward deck, now completely encrusted with coral and sponges— a favorite habitat for large fish. The entire superstructure is accessible, with entrances at the wheelhouse and at the

E. Both propellers are still mounted on the Thunderbolt *and have become encrusted with coral and sponge.*

F. Barracuda, Sphyraena barracuda, *are nearly always found in the wheelhouse.*

G. A spotted scorpionfish, Scorpaena plumieri, *waits for unsuspecting prey on the deck of the* Thunderbolt.

H. Bar jacks, Caranx ruber, *feed voraciously on zooplankton in the water column above the* Thunderbolt.

I. Starboard and underside of the Thunderbolt's *hull, overgrown with colorful encrusting sponges.*

level of the main deck. Swimming up the stairways inside is a strange experience. The bridge is normally inhabited by a school of barracuda, who occupy it in suspicious harmony with a school of grunts.

Farther aft, the engine compartments are open, allowing easy entry into the deepest part of the ship. Big schools of tiny silversides swirl all over this part of the ship, attracting the attention of black jacks and bar jacks that sweep through periodically to feed on them. At the stern the twin screws, coated with coral, are still exposed.

The *Thunderbolt* is located about 5 miles (8 kilometers) off Marathon. Depth on the wreck ranges from 75 feet (23 meters) at the top of the superstructure to 120 feet (36.6 meters) at the propellers. Visibility is usually 30 to 70 feet (9 to 21.3 meters), and even better when the position of the Gulf Stream is favorable. Currents vary and can be very strong at times.

Sombrero Reef and Delta Shoal

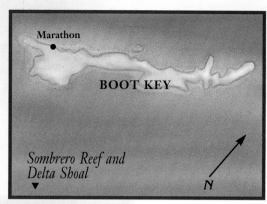

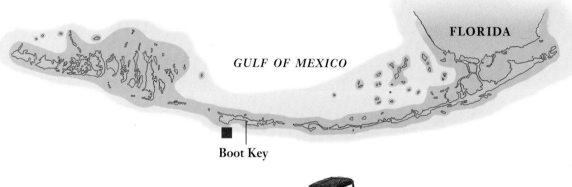

FLORIDA

GULF OF MEXICO

Boot Key

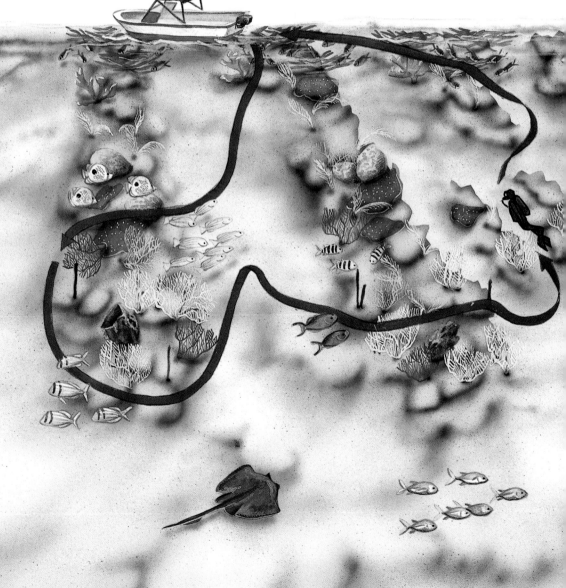

0 m
0 ft

1.5 m
5 ft

10.5 m
34 ft

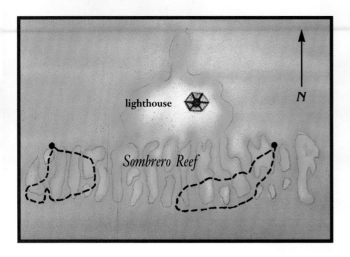

lighthouse

Sombrero Reef

N

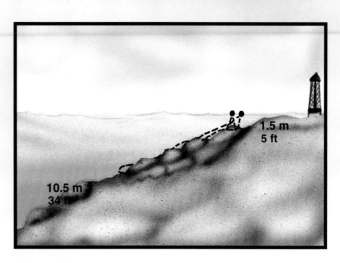

1.5 m
5 ft

10.5 m
34 ft

T his outer bank reef off Marathon is marked by one of the famous screw-pile lighthouses that were erected directly on the reefs during the mid-1850s. The Sombrero Key Lighthouse is the tallest of the reef lights at 160 feet (48.8 meters). Its construction, along with several other lighthouses in the Keys, was overseen by Lieutenant George Gordon Meade of the United States Army Corps of Topographical Engineers, who later rose to fame as commander of the Union Army during the American Civil War. Lieutenant Meade predicted that these lighthouses would last 200 years; after 140 years they are still structurally sound and carrying out their original function.

B

C

A

A. *The Sombrero Key Lighthouse is the tallest of the Forida Keys reef lights at 160 feet (49 meters).*

A. *The Sombrero Key Lighthouse is the tallest of the Forida Keys reef lights at 160 feet (49 meters).*

B. *A clear aerial view of the coral structure of Sombrero Reef.*

C. *Mixed schools of grunts on Sombrero Reef.*

D. *Yellowtail snappers, Ocyurus chrysurus, one of the most common snappers on Florida Keys reefs, and one of the boldest. Divers are likely to have yellowtails swim right up to them at any time.*

E. *Blue parrotfish, Scarus coeruleus, on Sombrero Reef at night.*

Like other outer bank reefs, the principal feature of Sombrero Reef is the spur-and-groove coral formations that extend from a depth of 5 feet (1.5 meters) to about 35 feet (10.6 meters). Topped with branches of elkhorn and staghorn coral and buttressed by boulders of star and brain coral, the parallel coral ridges form mini-canyons for divers. A favorite dive site is the Arch, where the coral limestone forms an interesting swim-through. Nurse sharks and southern stingrays are frequently encountered along the base of the ridges. Closer to the surface, the water above the coral is thick with colorfully striped sergeant majors and sleek bar jacks.

Delta Shoal is a nearby shallow reef that features the typical Florida Keys

D

E

spur-and-groove formations. As at Sombrero Reef, the fish are thick here, both in the water column and under the numerous ledges.

Sombrero Reef is located 4 nautical miles (7.4 kilometers) off Boot Key at the south end of Marathon. Delta Shoal is located less than 1 mile (1.6 kilometers) east of Sombrero Reef. Most diving is done between 15 and 35 feet (4.6 to 10.6 meters). Visibility varies from 30 to 60 feet (9 to 18.2 meters). Sombrero Reef is a Sanctuary Preservation Area, so exercise extra caution when diving or anchoring to avoid any damage to coral. Catch-and-release fishing is allowed in this area.

G

F

H

I

F. A parrotfish surrounded by its protective mucus cocoon at night on Sombrero Reef.

G. A squirrelfish, Holocentrus adscensionis, *next to pillar coral,* Dendrogyra cylindrus, *on Sombrero Reef.*

H. The peculiar body shape of a honeycomb cowfish, Lactophrys polygonia.

I. Queen angelfish, Holacanthus ciliaris, *one of the most colorful angelfish. Found on many Florida Keys reefs, where it dines frequently on sponges.*

Looe Key

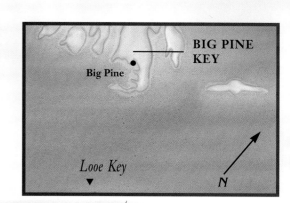

FLORIDA

GULF OF MEXICO

Big Pine Key

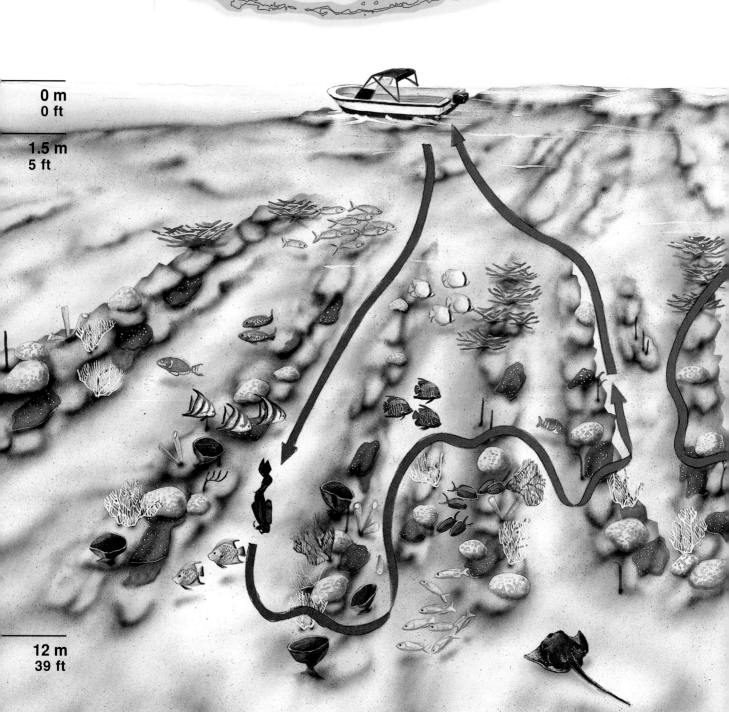

0 m
0 ft

1.5 m
5 ft

12 m
39 ft

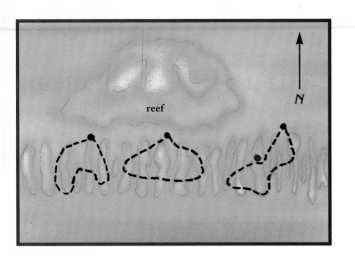

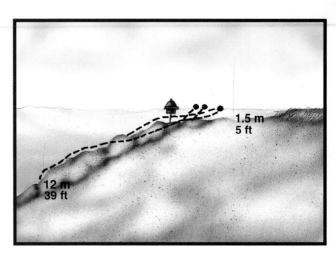

The Looe Key National Marine Sanctuary is a great underwater attraction in the Florida Keys. A complete ecosystem exists in this small coral community, named after a very special reef tract only 7 square miles (18.1 square kilometers) in area.

A rubble ridge, comprised mostly of fossilized corals deposited by storm surge, fascinates marine biologists. Sport divers and snorkelers enjoy examining the surrounding sea grass meadow. Sea grasses play a very important role in the health of the coral reef as a marine nursery, so you see the juveniles of many tropical reef fish species here. Large marine life, too, constantly passes through these shallows, including sharks, turtles, and the more common

A. An underwater photographer approaches one of the large brain corals at Looe Key.

B. Bluestriped grunts, Haemulon sciurus, *beneath a ledge on the Looe Key fore reef.*

C. An aerial view of Looe Key Reef shows in part the huge area designated National Marine Sanctuary.

D. A pair of logger-head turtles, Caretta caretta, *mating in the waters off Looe Key.*

stingrays. The outer bank reefs have proven most attractive for divers. Here spur-and-groove coral formations extend nearly a mile (1.6 kilometers) laterally. Mooring buoys are scattered throughout the Looe Key reef to prevent anchor damage from the thousands of boats that visit annually.

Because of the sanctuary's small size and potential for heavy tourist traffic, the Looe Key Reef was originally granted even more stringent protection than the Key Largo National Marine Sanctuary. Lobstering, which was allowed in Key Largo, was outlawed at Looe Key to prevent divers from overturning coral heads or crunching fragile polyps in their frantic pursuit of lobster. Because lobstering has been banned for many years at Looe Key, the population of these delectable invertebrates is impressive. Spear fishing is also banned, so the reef teems with life. Fish behave naturally here; they respond to the usual predators, feed on natural food, and reproduce in great numbers. You do not have to be a expert on

marine life to enjoy Looe Key—the proliferation of underwater life is a lesson in itself.

Looe Key is the epitome of Florida Keys outer bank reef. Its coral spurs are the tallest and thickest of all the reefs, with corals competing for every square inch of space. The diving is excellent from the shallow crest of the reef in only a few feet of water down to the deep reef at 105 feet (32 meters). Looe Key has been protected from spear fishing since 1981, so there are plenty of large predators, such as jacks and groupers, along with the small reef creatures on which they feed. But for its relatively remote location and variable visibility, Looe Key would take over Molasses Reef as the world's most visited dive site.

Looe Key is named for the *H.M.S. Looe,* which ran aground here in 1744. The reef is now marked with a navigation light and outlined by over 50 mooring buoys for diving and snorkeling. When the incoming tide brings clear water from the Gulf Stream, the reef sparkles beneath the sun. This is the place to bring all the camera gear you own because the opportunities for great photographs are endless. You will get great images whether you mount a 2:1 macrophotography tube on Nikonos V or a 16-mm ultrawide-angle lens in a housing.

The shallowest sections of the spurs are topped with golden brown branches of elkhorn coral. Be careful because the shallow water and constant wave action favor the growth of leafy fire coral that can leave a burning, itching patch on your skin. As the water gets deeper, the conditions change in favor of boulder corals—smooth brain coral, giant star coral, and starlet coral. In 20 to 30 feet (6 to 9 meters) of water at Looe Key there are star coral heads so large that they dominate the entire underwater landscape.

Boats leave for Looe Key from several locations between Bahia Honda and Ramrod Key. It is a journey of 7 to 10 nautical miles (13 to 18.5 kilometers). Most of the dive operations cluster around Big Pine Key. Diving on the

E. A school of Atlantic spadefish, Chaetodip-terus faber, *entertains a diver at Looe Key.*

F. A school of small-mouth grunts, Haemulon chrysar-gyreum, *swims along the top of a coral ridge in Looe Key.*

G. A surgeonfish at night on Looe Key fore reef.

H. Found on nearly all Florida Keys reefs, the rock beauty, Holacanthus tricolor, *is the shyest of the angelfish, generally hiding quickly if a diver approaches too closely.*

G

H

fore reef area involves depths from the surface to about 30 feet (9 meters). Visibility is usually 30 to 70 feet (9 to 21.3 meters), but can often be much better. The tidal cycle affects visibility at Looe Key more than at reefs in the Upper Keys. Currents at Looe Key are usually mild. Looe Key is a Sanctuary Preservation Area. Special regulations are in effect in these areas to ensure that the reef life is protected.

E

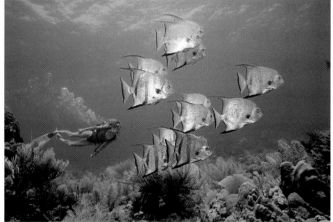

F

Looe Key Intermediate and Deep Reefs

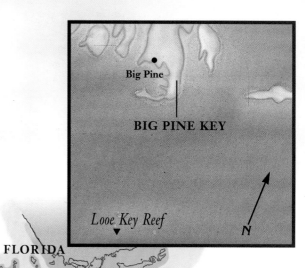

Big Pine

BIG PINE KEY

N

Looe Key Reef ▾

Big Pine Key

GULF OF MEXICO

FLORIDA

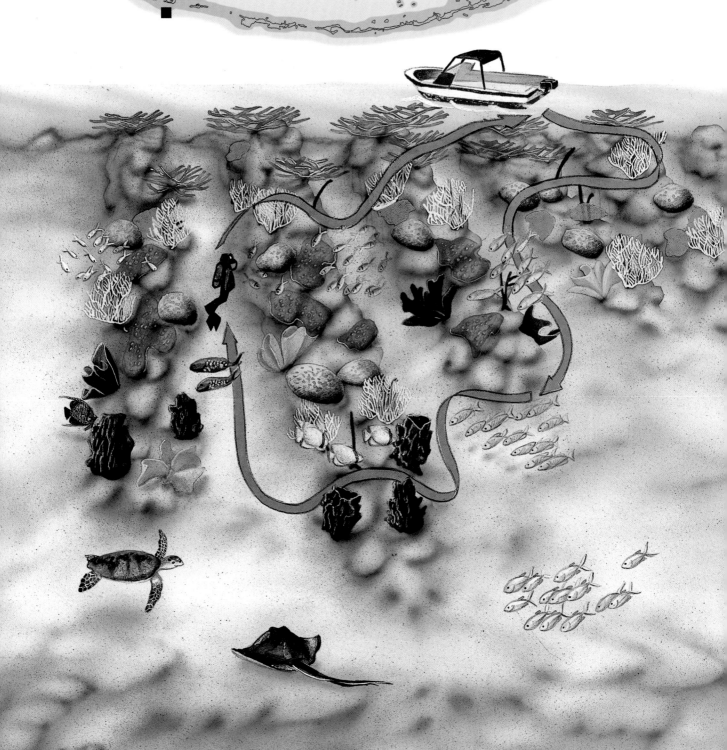

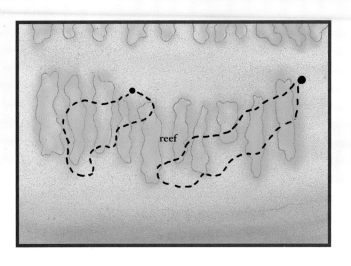

reef

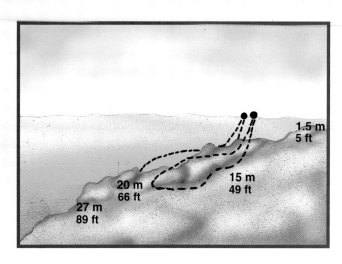

1.5 m
5 ft

20 m
66 ft

15 m
49 ft

27 m
89 ft

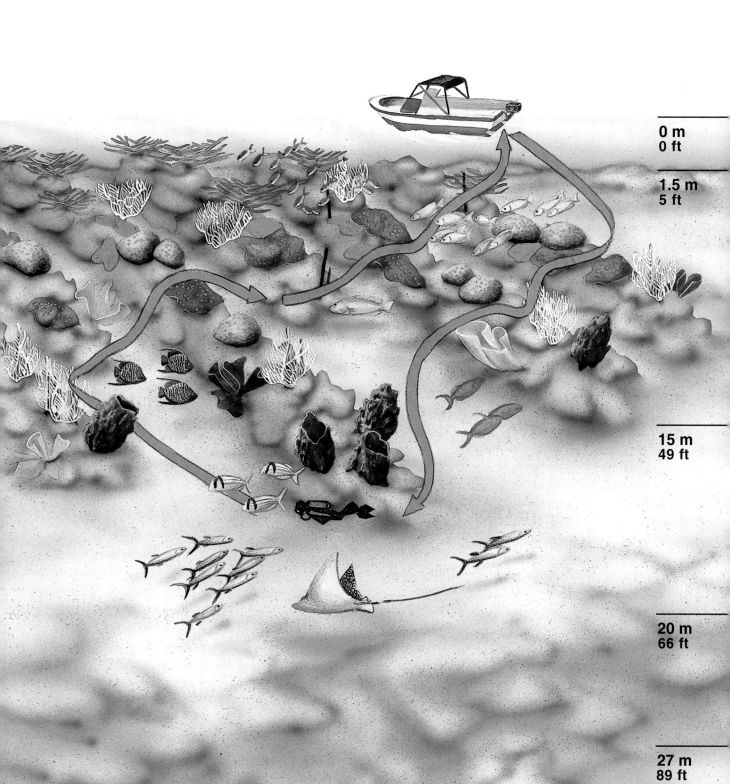

0 m
0 ft

1.5 m
5 ft

15 m
49 ft

20 m
66 ft

27 m
89 ft

A. The transition between the intermediate and deep reefs is marked in part by the increasing presence of barrel sponges, Xestospongia muta.

B. Deepwater sea fans, Iciligorgia schrammi, provide shelter for a trumpetfish, Aulostomus maculatus, on the deep reef.

If you plan to make 2 consecutive dives on Looe Key, start at one of the moorings on the deeper part of the reef. These are located in 50 to 60 feet (15.2 to 18.2 meters) of water, right along the boundary of the intermediate and deep reefs. These are not hard boundaries under water, but they generally describe reef areas that are distinctly different from the spur-and-groove formations in the main reef.

The intermediate reef begins in about 35 feet (10.6 meters) of water,

where the coral spurs begin to taper off. From this point the vertical profile of the coral is less distinct and the sand channels begin to wander a bit compared to their straight runs in shallower water. The seascape looks like a plain covered with sea fans, sea rods, and smaller hard corals. Sponges begin to crop up more frequently. There is also a rise in the number of fish that feed directly on the reef, such as parrotfish, who eat coral, and angelfish, who eat sponges.

You can tell you have moved from the intermediate reef to the deep reef by the number and size of the barrel sponges. Sponges generally grow well at this depth; you may notice many more gray tube sponges, red finger sponges, brown tube sponges, and orange boring sponges. Deepwater sea fans grow in more abundance. too. As you near the 65-foot (19.8-meter) mark, the reef slopes more steeply. This is a good place to watch for larger creatures, such as spotted eagle rays, reef sharks, and green sea turtles.

Depths in the Looe Key interme-

C. A hawksbill turtle, Eretmochelys imbricata, swims over the low coral and sea fans typical of the intermediate reef.

D. Queen angelfish, Holacanthus ciliaris, in the transition area between the intermediate and deep reefs.

E. A stoplight parrot-fish, Sparisoma viride, *assumes an unusual coloration while resting in an orange elephant ear sponge,* Agelas clathrodes, *on the deep reef.*

F. Midnight parrot-fish, Scarus coelestinus, *at night in the shallowest part of the intermediate reef.*

diate and deep reef areas range from 40 to just over 100 feet (12.2 to 30.4 meters). As in the fore reef area, visibility is usually 30 to 70 feet (9 to 21.3 meters), but varies with the tides and is frequently in the 50-to-90-foot (15.2-to-27.4-meter) range. Currents can be somewhat higher in the deep reef, but are still usually mild to moderate. As with the fore reef, the intermediate and deep reefs are included in the Looe Key Sanctuary Preservation Area.

H

E

F

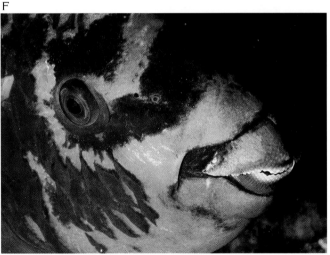

G

I

G. Nurse shark, Ginglymostoma cirratum, *in a narrow sand channel in the deep reef.*

H. The gray angelfish, Pomacanthus arcuatus, *is one of the symbols of the Florida Keys waters.*

I. This foureye butter-flyfish, Chaetodon capistratus, *seems to look for protection in the intermediate reef.*

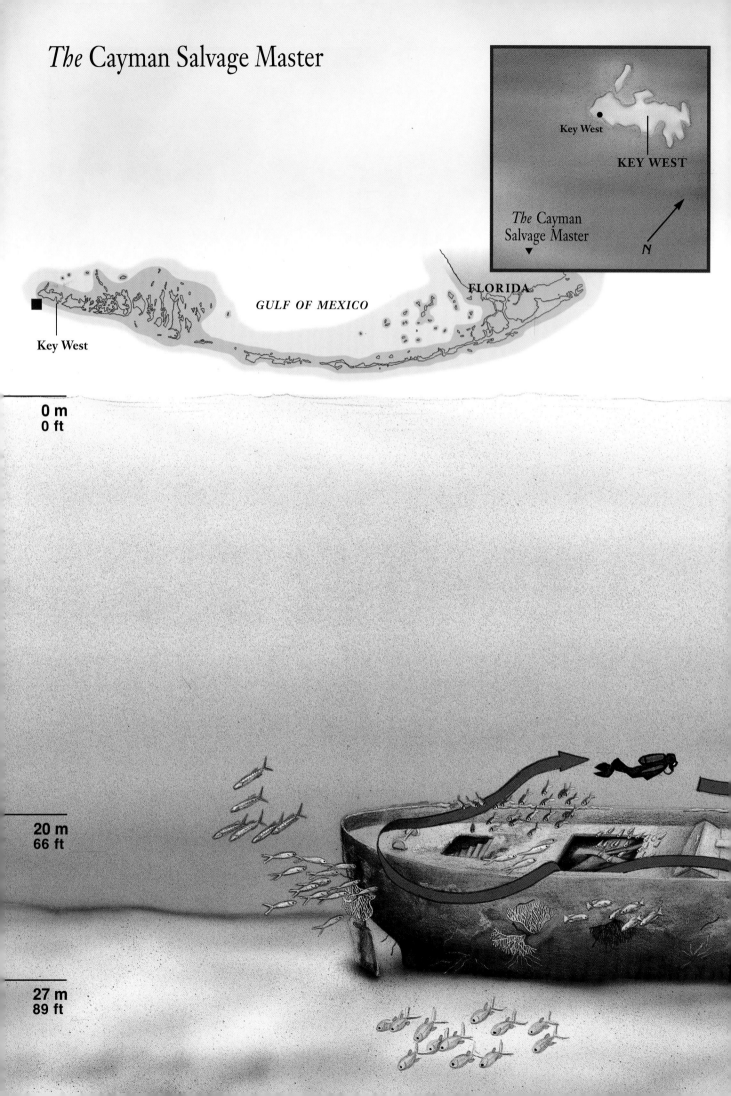

The Cayman Salvage Master

KEY WEST

The Cayman
Salvage Master

N

GULF OF MEXICO

FLORIDA

Key West

Key West

0 m
0 ft

20 m
66 ft

27 m
89 ft

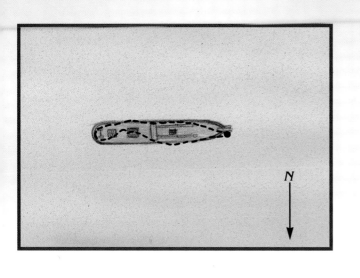

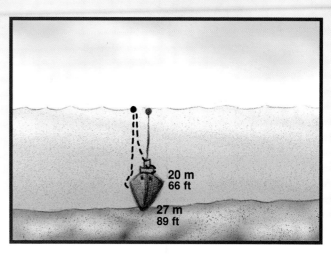

20 m
66 ft

27 m
89 ft

A

Originally built as a United States Coast Guard buoy tender in 1936, the *Cayman Salvage Master* was first converted to lay cable and later to be a Panamanian freighter. The vessel transported refugees in the 1980 Mariel boat lift from Cuba, an illegal act that resulted in its seizure by the government. The *Cayman Salvage Master* languished in the outer mole of the Truman Annex in Key West from 1980 to 1983, eventually sinking at the dock. After it was raised, the pilot house was removed and the vessel was designated for sinking as a sport fishing attraction in 300 feet (91.4 meters) of water. On the way to the disposal site in April of 1985, however, the *Cayman*

B

D

C

Salvage Master sank prematurely, landing on her port side in 90 feet (27.4 meters) of water about 4 miles (6.4 kilometers) south of Key West. In one of those rare benevolent acts of nature, Hurricane Katrina turned the vessel upright later that year. The pilot house that was removed prior to the sinking was later used to establish an artificial reef in 60 feet (18.2 meters) of water on the Gulf of Mexico side of Key West.

The *Cayman Salvage Master* is 187 feet (57 meters) long with a beam of 37 feet (11.3 meters). Even though the superstructure was removed, the vessel still rises 26 feet (8 meters) from the bottom, attracting a cloud of fish and providing lots of growing space for coral. The entire starboard side is covered with swaying soft corals. The large cable spool is still attached to the bow and is the focal point for a large school of fish. This cable spool is very different from the one on the bow of the *Thunderbolt*. The *Cayman Salvage Master*'s spool is designed solely to guide the cable over the bow, rather than store any of it aboard. A large set of bits are still mounted to the aft deck, but the propeller has been removed.

Although there are several openings along the deck, the *Cayman Salvage Master* is best enjoyed from the outside. Just swimming from one end to the other will occupy most of the allowable no-decompression limits on a dive,

so relax and enjoy the tremendous numbers of fish that are attracted to the wreck.

The *Cayman Salvage Master* is located about 6 miles (1.8 kilometers) south of Key West. Depths range from 67 feet (20.4 meters) to the deck to 90 feet (27.4 meters) on the sand at the stern of the vessel. Visibility is usually between 30 and 70 feet (9 and 21.3 meters), but can often be 80 to 100 feet (24.3 to 30.4 meters). Frequent strong currents make this an advanced dive.

A. Part of the bow of *the* Cayman Salvage Master, *sunk in 1985.*

B. *The* Cayman Salvage Master *was a 187-foot (57-meter) vessel sunk in 90 feet (27 meters) of water off Key West.*

C. *A diver in the background and the stern of the* Cayman Salvage Master *in foreground.*

D. *A diver inspects the cable reel on the bow of the* Cayman Salvage Master.

E. *Rich underwater life surrounds the wrecks. Here is a reef octopus,* Octopus briareus.

F. *A sleek permit,* Trachinotus falcatus, *sweeps past the deck of the* Cayman Salvage Master.

G. *Hawksbill turtles,* Eretmochelys imbricata, *are sometimes spotted on the wreck of the* Cayman Salvage Master.

H. *The* Cayman Salvage Master *acts as an artificial reef and provides shelter for numerous green moray eels,* Gymnothorax funebris, *which can be seen at almost any time of day.*

I. *Nassau groupers,* Epinephelus striatus, *often visit divers on the structures of the* Cayman Salvage Master.

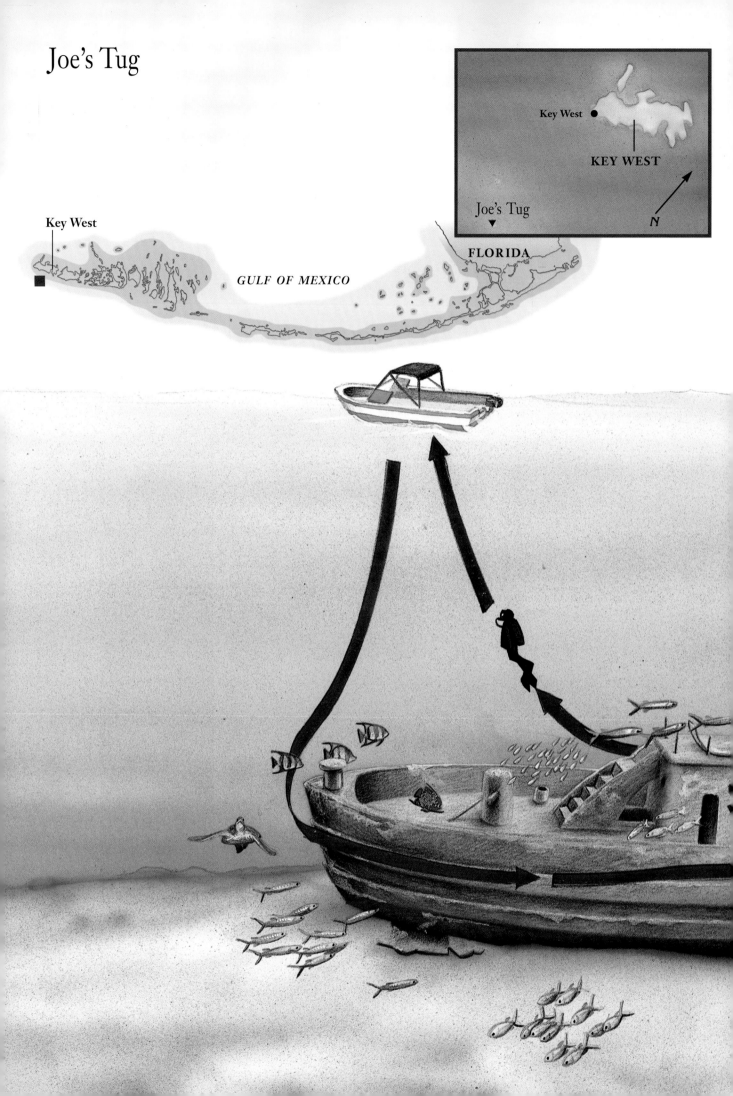

Joe's Tug

GULF OF MEXICO

Key West

FLORIDA

Key West

KEY WEST

Joe's Tug

N

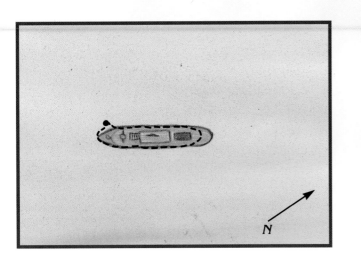

A

B

C

This 75-foot (23-meter) harbor tug ended up on the bottom 6 miles (9.7 kilometers) from Key West. Popular lore suggests that this was the result of a midnight raid by a local character named Joe and his friends on the evening before the vessel was to be towed north. The boat had sunk at the pier in Key West's Safe Harbor in 1986 and was raised with the intention of making it into an artificial reef off Miami. After it had been cleaned and prepped, however, it was surreptitiously taken out of the Key West harbor and sunk during the night. But everything did not go exactly as planned during the caper, and the boat sank a bit prematurely, landing on a portion of the reef.

D

For several years there was very little diving on the wreck, partly because no one wanted to be associated too closely with the escapade. It was "rediscovered" as a dive site around 1990, and has become increasingly popular since then. The tug rests now in 65 feet (20 meters) of water, sitting upright and largely intact, although a tropical storm removed the wheelhouse from the top of the cabin superstructure some years ago. A large jewfish and a big green moray eel are habitually found on the wreck, along with a population of great barracuda, blue angelfish, schoolmasters, and occasional hawksbill turtles.

The entire interior of the boat, from cabin to engine compartment, is open.

A. Joe's Tug, a 75-foot (23-meter) harbor tug sunk in 65 feet (20 meters) of water off Key West in 1986.

B. A diver closely observes the bow of the tug on a sandy bottom.

C. The wreck of Joe's Tug is inhabited by many fish, who enjoy its shelter and protection.

D. The big rudder of Joe's Tug is still attached, but the propeller was removed before sinking.

E. After more than a decade on the sea bottom the hull is well coated with encrusting coral and sponge.

F. Schoolmasters, Lutjanus apodus, and a variety of other grunts take shelter during the day within the wreckage of Joe's Tug.

G. Juvenile Caesar grunts, Haemulon carbonarium, inhabit the remains of the superstructure.

H. Turtles, such as this loggerhead, Caretta caretta, are often seen on Joe's Tug.

The combination of this easy access and the relatively shallow depth makes *Joe's Tug* a good site for a diver at any level of expertise. The interior compartments are packed with French and bluestriped grunts, which tolerate a very close approach from divers. A couple of barracuda are nearly always in the favored position at the top of the cabin. The big rudder still hangs from the stern, covered now with encrusting coral. The propeller was removed before the ship was sunk, but the broad overhang of the tug's stern provides shelter for large numbers of fish. This is a productive place for photographers, as are the bow and the pilothouse.

F

E

G

Joe's Tug is about 6 nautical miles (11.1 kilometers) south of Key West. Depths on the wreck range from 40 feet (12.2 meters) at the cabin to 65 feet (19.8 meters) at the bottom of the rudder. Visibility is usually 30 to 70 feet (9 to 21.3 meters), frequently better. Currents can vary day to day, but are usually not as strong as on deeper wrecks.

H

Nine Foot Stake

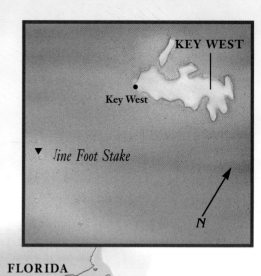

KEY WEST

Key West

▼ *Nine Foot Stake*

N

Key West

GULF OF MEXICO

FLORIDA

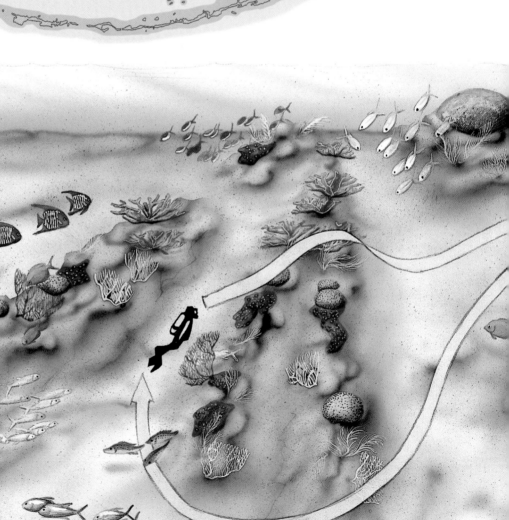

0 m
0 ft

3 m
10 ft

7.5 m
25 ft

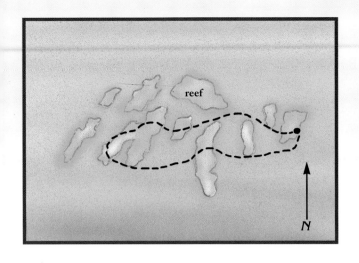

reef

N

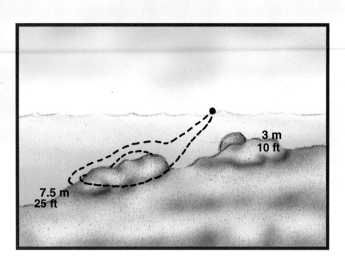

3 m
10 ft

7.5 m
25 ft

A. An enormous boulder brain coral, Colpophylia natans, *is one of the dominant features of this shallow reef.*

B. A variety of hard and soft corals compete for space on the exposed hard bottom.

C. A magnificent feather duster, Sabellastarte magnifica, *grows from a boulder brain coral,* Colpophylia natans, *on Nine Foot Stake.*

The centerpiece of the shallow reef called Nine Foot Stake is an enormous hemisphere of smooth brain coral. The top of the formation is in only 10 feet (3 meters) of water and the bottom is braced on a coral ledge that has been severely undercut. Viewed from the top the coral looks completely unblemished and nearly round. From the bottom, though, it is more like a bubble than a globe. Given that this species of coral grows about 1 centimeter (less than .5 inch) a year, its 7-to-10-foot (2-to-3-meter) diameter makes it centuries old.

The maximum depth at Nine Foot

A

B

C

D

E

Stake is 25 feet (7.6 meters). The reef structure consists of coral mounds scattered across a sand and coral rubble bottom. The mounds rise up as much as 12 feet (3.7 meters) from the bottom, making this a good site for both divers and snorkelers. The mounds are undercut in many places, providing excellent protected areas for reef fish. Blue tangs, Spanish hogfish, and yellow goatfish are common on the reef. Large predator fish, such as permit and Crevalle jacks, cruise by frequently.

D. A squirrelfish, Holocentrus adscensionis, *swims close to the incredible coral formations on Nine Foot Stake.*

E. Many colored fish, such as this porkfish, Anisotremus virginicus, *can be seen during dives on Nine Foot Stake.*

F. Bluestriped grunts,
Haemulon sciurus,
closely packed in the
shelter of an undercut
coral ledge on Nine
Foot Stake.

G. Southern stingrays,
Dasyatis americana,
can be seen at night on
the sandy bed at Nine
Foot Stake.

Nine Foot Stake is also visited regularly for night dives, because it is shallow and close to Key West Harbor. Photographers should set up for close-up or macrophotography on these dives. The reef comes alive at night with hundreds of small creatures—hermit crabs, nudibranches, anemones, and brittle stars.

Nine Foot Stake is located about 4 nautical miles (7.4 kilometers) south of Key West. Depths range between the surface and 15 feet (4.6 meters). Visibility is usually 25 to 50 feet (7.6 to 15.2 meters). Currents are usually very mild.

H

F

I

G

H. Horse-eye jacks,
Caranx latus,
provide a stunning
encounter, especially
for photographers who
catch their silver
coloring against the
blue depths.

I. Blue tangs, Acanthurus coeruleus,
are typical reef fish
and can be frequently
seen during dives at
Nine Foot Stake.

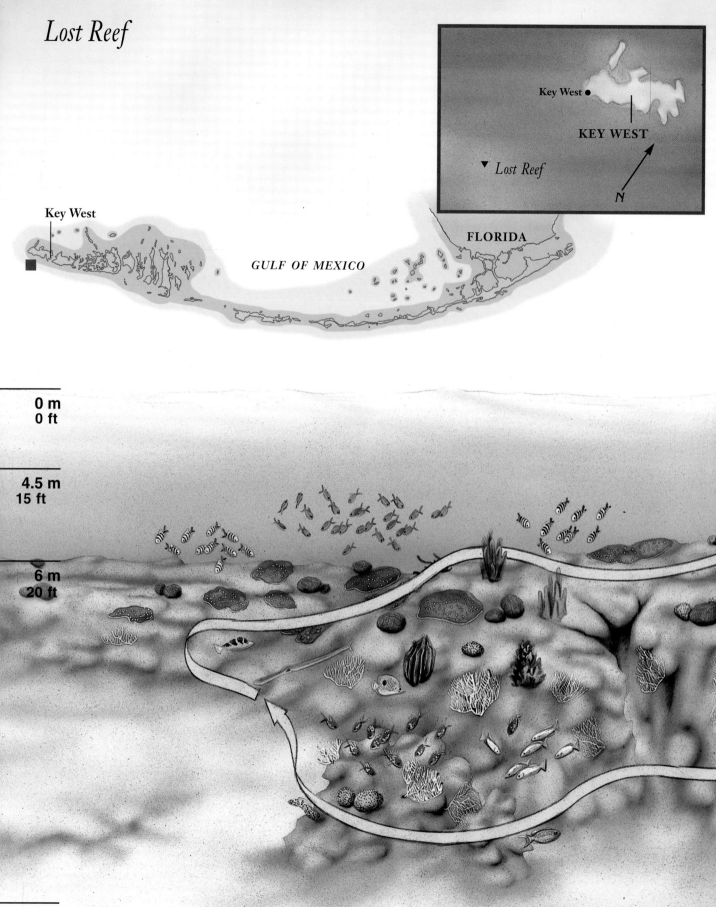

Lost Reef

KEY WEST

Lost Reef

N

Key West

GULF OF MEXICO

FLORIDA

0 m
0 ft

4.5 m
15 ft

6 m
20 ft

21 m
69 ft

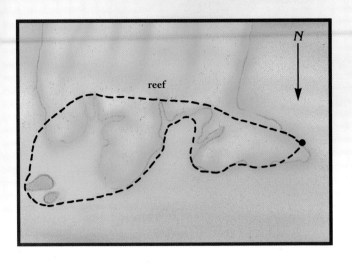

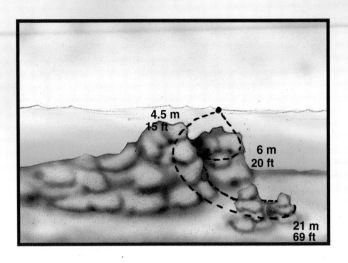

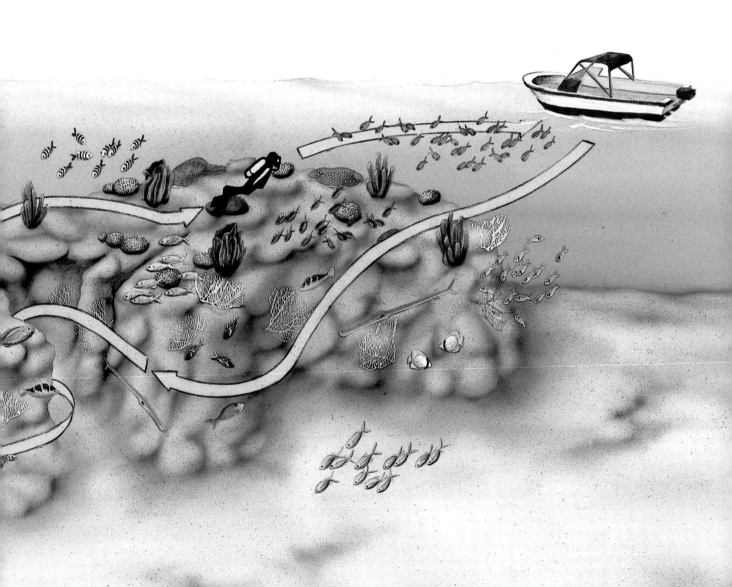

A. A pair of spotfin butterflyfish, Chaetodon ocellatus, *stays in front of a porous sea rod,* Pseudoplexaura sp., *on the shallow side of the reef.*

B. Several large colonies of pillar coral, Dendrogyra cylindrus, *can be found on Lost Reef.*

A 6-to-10-foot (1.8-to-3-meter) ledge snakes around the back of Lost Reef, undercut in places with caverns and split with narrow canyons. Schools of fish are sometimes packed beneath the ledge so tightly that 5 or more species mingle. The ledge continues along nearly the entire length of the north side, and the reef has a modified spur-and-groove formation on the south side. The water is deeper to the south, where the reef maintains a

B

A

C

D

C. A hawksbill turtle, Eretmochelys imbricata, *swims over the sandy back reef area of Lost Reef.*

D. French angelfish, Pomacanthus paru, *are often seen in pairs on Lost Reef.*

gradual slope from 20 feet (6 meters) downward. On the north side the reef ends abruptly at a ledge with a sandy bottom dotted with occasional hard and soft corals.

The water over the reef is filled with fish, including hundreds of blue chromis, Creole wrasses, and sergeant majors, feeding on the microscopic organisms. Closer to the reef, the population changes to trumpetfish, squirrelfish, and balloonfish, which take advantage of the reef for cover. Large numbers of midnight and stoplight parrotfish also swim along the reef, staying close to their food source.

Lost Reef is a dive that is best not hurried. There is too much territory to cover on 1 or even 2 dives, so relax and enjoy exploring one small section of the reef at a time. Moving slowly gives you time to discover the spotted moray eels that hide under the coral and the gobies that burrow in the sand.

Lost Reef is located about 7 nautical miles (13 kilometers) southwest of Key West. Depths range from 15 to 70 feet (4.6 to 21.3 meters), with the best coral cover between 20 and 40 feet (6 to 12.2 meters). Visibility is usually 25 to 70 feet (7.6 to 21.3 meters), and currents tend to be very mild.

E

F

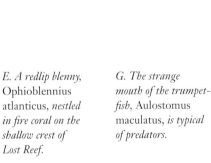

E. A redlip blenny, Ophioblennius atlanticus, *nestled in fire coral on the shallow crest of Lost Reef.*

F. This balloonfish, Diodon holocanthus, *was found in one of the sand channels on the front of Lost Reef.*

G. The strange mouth of the trumpetfish, Aulostomus maculatus, *is typical of predators.*

G

Western Dry Rocks

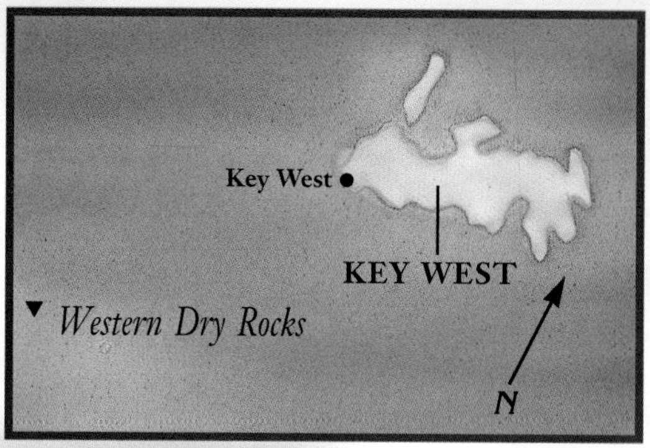

Key West

FLORIDA

GULF OF MEXICO

Key West ●

KEY WEST

▼ *Western Dry Rocks*

N

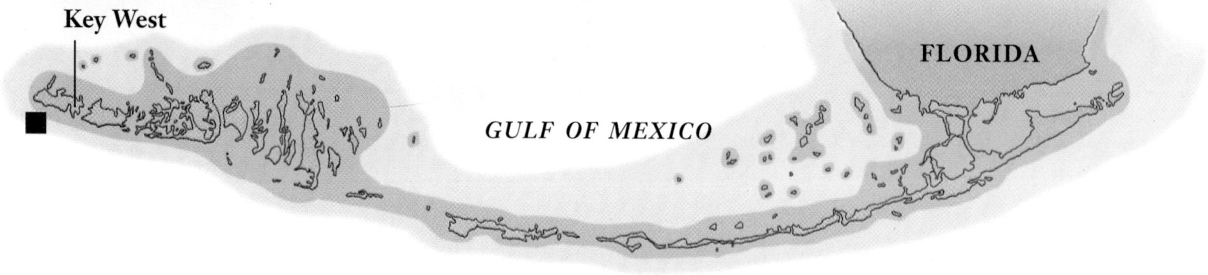

0 m	
0 ft	
3 m	
10 ft	
7.5 m	
25 ft	
13.5 m	
44 ft	
↓ 30 m	
98 ft	

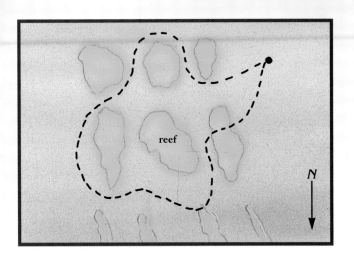

reef

N

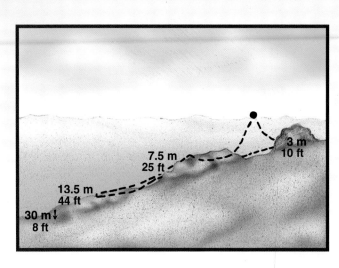

7.5 m
25 ft

13.5 m
44 ft

3 m
10 ft

30 m↓
8 ft

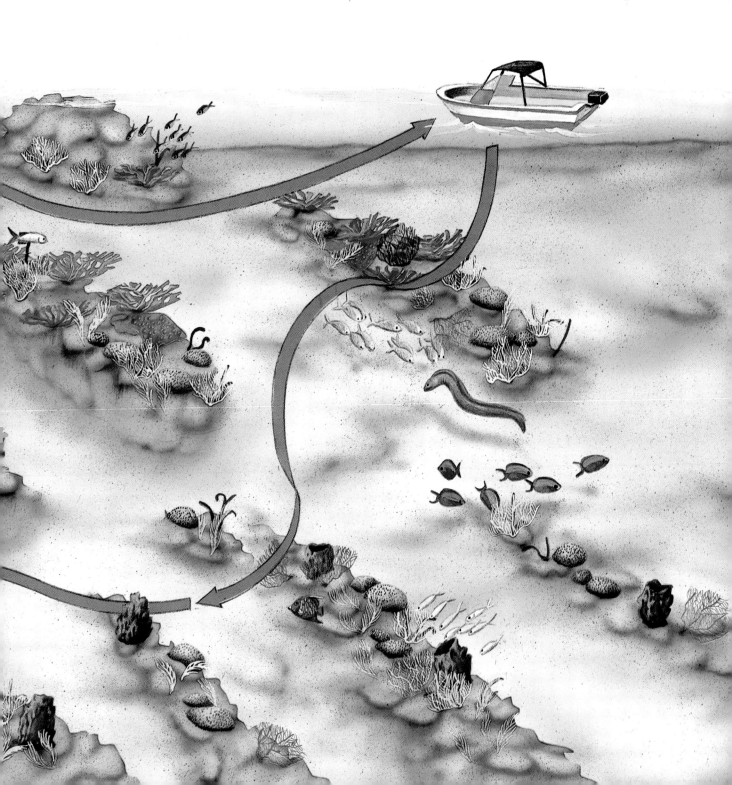

A

B

C

D

E

W estern Dry Rocks is a large, sprawling reef frequently visited by dive charter boats in Key West. The shallowest part of the reef breaks the surface at low tide and slopes to over 100 feet (30.4 meters) before the living coral gets too sparse. The shallowness of the reef and its position relative to land make it a good reef for diving and snorkeling in almost any weather. Whatever the wind direction, there is generally a protected side of the reef.

Coral heads grow on Western Dry

Rocks as if they had been cultivated. Healthy mounds of brain coral and star coral are almost evenly spaced along the reef, as though the whole seascape had been carefully planned. Heads of smooth starlet coral and convoluted brain coral are also scattered here and there. As the water gets deeper, the coral heads get larger and older. Some of the most ancient mounds of star coral, which have been alive for about 300 years, are obviously entering their twilight. Orange boring sponges have invaded their calcium carbonate skele-

A. Elkhorn coral, Acropora palmata, *characterizes the shallow coral spurs at Western Dry Rocks.*

B. Atlantic spadefish, Chaetodipterus faber, *cross the blue waters of Western Dry Rocks.*

C. A school of small-mouth grunts, Haemulon chrysargyreum, *swims past shallow sea fans on Western Dry Rocks.*

D. A colorful peppermint goby, Coryphopterus lipernes, *perches on brain coral in the shallows at Western Dry Rocks.*

E. A diver swims over a large colony of boulder brain coral, Colpophylia natans, *on the shallow back side of Western Dry Rocks.*

F. Butter hamlets, Hypoplectrus unicolor, *are a common sight on night dives on Western Dry Rocks.*

G. Spotfin butterfly-fish, Chaetodon ocellatus, *at Western Dry Rocks. Like many of the butterflyfish species, spotfins are normally seen in pairs.*

tons, lifting their edges like curling shingles. Their bases have been eroded by time, giving them the appearance of giant mushrooms on the bottom. These venerable coral heads have become even more beautiful in their old age. For fish on the reef, these coral heads are like the old oak tree in a village square—a spot where everyone comes to meet. They are surrounded by fish and provide habitat for thousands of invertebrates. If you are carrying a camera, spend some time around these elder statesmen of the reef. They provide good photographic opportunities for nearly any lens.

Western Dry Rocks is an excellent site for both divers and snorkelers. Beginning divers find the navigation easy and the depths moderate. Advanced divers appreciate the size of the reef and the numerous caves and undercut ledges. It is easy for buddy pairs to make the whole dive without running into other divers. The shallow water and usually calm seas are great for snorkelers.

H

I

F

G

The bold yellow-and-black colors of porkfish and the bright royal blue of the blue parrotfish are only part of the color palette at Western Dry Rocks. True to the reputation of the Florida Keys as a dive destination rich in fish, this reef is home to hundreds of species of reef fish. Bluehead wrasses, green moray eels, yellowtail snappers, and blue tangs are just a few of the commonly seen reef fish. Western Dry Rocks also attracts some of the larger fish. Nurse sharks and bull sharks are seen here frequently.

Western Dry Rocks is about 8 nautical miles (15 kilometers) southwest of Key West. Depths on most dives range from the surface to around 45 feet (13.7 meters), with much of the best coral and fish life between 10 and 25 feet (3 and 7.6 meters). Visibility is usually 25 to 70 feet (7.6 to 21.4 meters), but can exceed 80 feet (24.3 meters). Currents are usually very mild.

H. The many coral crevices along the back of Western Dry Rocks offer excellent habitats for species such as the squirrel-fish, Holocentrus adscensionis.

I. Nurse sharks, Ginglymostoma cirratum, *can usually be observed resting beneath the shallow ledge at Western Dry Rocks.*

THE FISH OF THE FLORIDA KEYS

The over 200 islands that make up the Florida Keys extend the Florida peninsula, like the beads of a coral necklace, into the Straits of Florida. They are the result of a long interaction with the sea, the corals, and the sediments that surround them. Exposed to atmospheric agents, rain, and sun, corals were eroded, their limestone dissolved and transformed into a sort of natural cement that compacted the entire surrounding sea floor. The whole process was the work of glaciers, which transformed the waters of the planet into ice, thereby removing liquid mass from the oceans. Then, in the now familiar cycle of alternating warm and cold periods, the sea once again prevailed and covered the modified islands, which were again colonized by innumerable living beings. New corals grew on ancient fossil corals, turning into solid rock on contact with air, and the sea floor was repopulated with fish, sponges, and gorgonians, in forms that were both ancient and new. Thus, bit by bit, the Florida Keys were created, aided by the vast, relatively shallow sea beds that make up the bay of Florida. To the west the bay is delimited by the relatively shallow (about 2,625 feet [800 meters]) Straits of Florida, through which the Florida current flows at a speed of 2 to 4 miles (3 to 7 kilometers) an hour, carrying the waters of the Caribbean toward the Atlantic. Transformed into a sort of peninsula by the numerous bridges that join the principal islands between Angelfish Creek and Key West (the southernmost part of the United States), the Florida Keys became an attraction for thousands of divers from the United States and abroad. Their gradual discovery of these now famous sea beds played a role in creating the sport of diving. Some of the things that divers find so attractive about the Keys include the warm water, abundant life, and good visibility, which is not always constant but in general is at least 50 to 80 feet (15 to 25 meters), in some areas increasing to an estimated 165 feet (50 meters). In some places, the reefs on which the islands of the archipelago are located extend in a band as wide as 36 feet (11 kilometers). This band contains numerous environments that, starting from the areas closest to the coast, provide a microcosm of all the habitats of the Caribbean. Along the shores of the Florida peninsula and many of its islands there are large mangrove forests, varying in size depending on the rhythm of the tides. These are extremely fragile environments, which are becoming increasingly rare due to the extent to which human beings have altered the delicate balance between the waters and sediments on which they depend. An exploration of these areas, which are generally popular with bird-watching fans, can hold extraordinary surprises for divers. Many fish species can be discovered here, primarily the young of many coralline fish usually found farther out to sea. In the shallower sandy areas there are vast meadows of phanerogams—not unlike the Neptune grass of the Mediterranean—which provide ideal environments for the reproduction of many species. Where the currents or the depth prevents these plants from colonizing, the first corals appear. Isolated blocks of hard corals sometimes thrust up to the surface, breaking the monotony of the sandy sea floors where goatfish, trunkfish, silversides, triggerfish, and small parrotfish swim.

As you leave the coastline and the inner reef, you will note that the color of the sea changes, alternating dark blue and lighter patches. This change in color is the result of corresponding changes in the sea floor, where corals are the primary element. Hard corals, including staghorn, brain, or columnar corals, grow luxuriantly and create diverse habitats. Caves, coral masses, and channels with sandy floors make this portion of the coastal area particularly interesting. The sand channels that interrupt the reef are a prelude to broad stretches of fine sediments, followed by deep secondary reefs that only more experienced divers should attempt to explore. Man's long habitation of this area has certainly changed the environment, but not as much as might be expected. Dives are strictly regulated and are permitted only in established sites marked by various types of buoys, depending on the area. There are numerous marine parks and protected areas. Pennekamp Park (the largest marine park in the United States, established in 1960), the Key Largo National Marine Sanctuary, and the Florida Keys National Marine Sanctuary are protected and strictly regulated areas.

In the Florida Keys you can discover abundant formations of staghorn corals, some in the form of walls, in the shadow of which are sweepers, grunts, and soldierfish. All around, you will frequently see large barrel

sponges and gorgonians, both sea fans and feather or branch gorgonians. The gorgonians are the most conspicuous of the benthic organisms, enlivened and rendered almost mobile by numerous fish, from little gobies that seem illuminated from within, to morays, groupers, and snappers. In the open waters there are often tarpon and carangids, which may suddenly open their ranks to reveal the disquieting but harmless presence of a large barracuda or a group of majestic mantas. To list all the species here would be an impossible task and would certainly fail to do justice to these waters, which, owing to their special position as a transition point from the continent to the heart of the Caribbean, have just as many tropical as temperate-water species, making them a colorful and fascinating environment.

CARCHARHINIDAE FAMILY

Tiger shark
Galeocerdo cuvieri

Short, wide nose; upper lobe of caudal fin larger than lower. Blue-gray coloring, with dark vertical bars more visible in the young. Extremely dangerous and often found in coastal, even brackish, waters. Seen along outer reef walls and offshore barriers. Grows up to 18 feet (5.5 meters) long. Found in all the circumtropical seas.

GINGLYMOSTOMATIDAE FAMILY

Nurse shark
Ginglymostoma cirratum

Straight body flattened along the belly; close-set dorsal fins; small mouth with two short barbels on underside of head. Yellow-gray coloring. Lives on sandy sea beds between reefs, sheltered by big corals and caves. Grows up to 14 feet (4 meters) long. Found from Rhode Island to Brazil.

DASYATIDAE FAMILY

Southern stingray
Dasyatis americana

Lozenge-shaped body, more or less pronounced; pointed nose; slightly pointed pectoral fins. A line of tubercles runs down the center of the back; a long sharp spine in the front half of the tail. Tends to bury itself in the sand when resting on the sea bed. Gray-black coloring, lighter in the young. Reaches a width of 5 feet (1.5 meters). Found from New Jersey to Brazil.

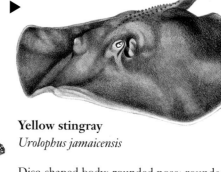

Yellow stingray
Urolophus jamaicensis

Disc-shaped body; rounded nose; rounded pectoral fin tips. The short tail has poisonous spines at the tip. Yellow-brown coloring with dark markings of varying size. Lives on sandy sea beds, where it buries itself close to the reefs. Can measure up to 30 inches (76 centimeters) in width. Found from North Carolina to Venezuela.

MOBULIDAE FAMILY

Manta ray
Manta birostris

Certainly the best-known representative of the rays; easily recognizable by its large pectoral fins transformed into wings. Characteristic mobile cephalic fins convey into its mouth the plankton on which it feeds. Often observed in small groups swimming near the surface, where it allows the tips of its wings to emerge from the water. Its back is black; its underside, pure white with black spots. May reach 22 feet (6.7 meters) in width.

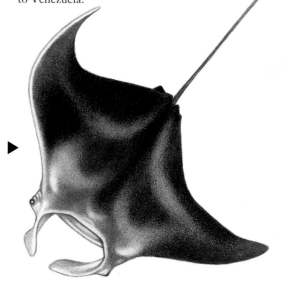

MYLIOBATIDAE FAMILY

Spotted eagle ray
Aetobatus narinari

Lozenge-shaped body; big, pointed wings; pointed, convex head. The tail is almost 3 times as long as the body and has toothed spines along it. The back is dark in coloring with numerous light spots. Lives in deep reef channels close to shady beds. Grows up to 8 feet (2.5 meters) in width. Found in circumtropical waters.

TORPEDINIDAE FAMILY

Lesser electric ray
Narcine brasiliensis

Anterior portion disk-shaped, narrowing to a medium-length tail surmounted by two dorsal fins. Its eyes are in a dorsal position. Two bean-shaped electric organs, located at the side of its head, can be seen against the light. Its color varies from gray to reddish, with a few round spots. It lives on sandy sea beds to a depth of 98 to 131 feet (30 to 40 meters). Grows up to 18 inches (46 centimeters) long. Its shock is weak and not dangerous to humans. Found from the Caribbean to Argentina.

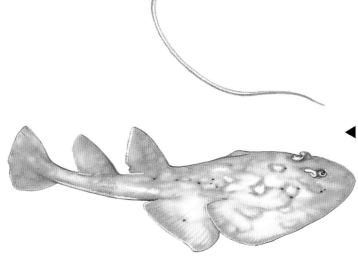

MURAENIDAE FAMILY

Green moray
Gymnothorax funebris

Easily identified by its green color, which varies in intensity from specimen to specimen, but is always uniform. Nocturnal; hides in reef crevices, often in shallow water, during the day. Can be easily approached, but may attack when provoked. Grows up to 7.5 feet (over 2 meters) long. Found from Florida to Brazil.

Chain moray
Echidna catenata

Powerful body, tall and compressed at the back; short head; dorsal fin starts behind the bronchial opening. Yellow coloring with lighter chain-shaped pattern; yellow eyes. Prefers shallow, rocky, coral sea beds with abundant crevices where it can hide. Grows up to 20 inches (50 centimeters) long. Found from Florida to Brazil.

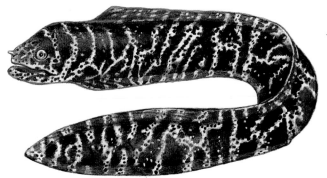

Spotted moray
Gymnothorax moringa

Common in shallow sea beds rich in vegetation, where it hides in crevices during the day, coming out at night to hunt. Yellow-white coloring with numerous brown or red-black markings. Can grow up to 5 feet (1.5 meters) long. Found from South Carolina to Brazil.

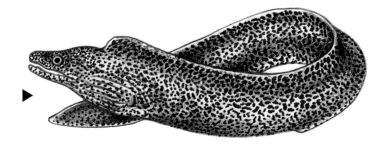

Goldentail moray

Gymnothorax miliaris

Small tapered body; slightly pointed head. It is nocturnal; by day takes refuge among the crevices of the coral reefs from a few meters to over 197 feet (60 meters) in depth. Brownish body dotted with small yellow spots. Its tail is golden yellow and its eyes are edged with yellow. Grows up to 27 inches (60 centimeters) long. Found from Florida to Brazil and around the islands of the Atlantic.

CONGRIDAE FAMILY

Brown garden eel

Heteroconger halis

Elongated body and tapered head with large eyes and small mouth. Grayish brown. Lives in colonies on sandy sea beds, where it always stays buried, leaving only its mouth and a portion of its body exposed. Grows up to 24 inches (60 centimeters) long. Found throughout the Caribbean.

MEGALOPIDAE FAMILY

Tarpon

Megalops atlanticus

Big, robust body; oblique, upturned mouth. Silvery body covered in large scales. Last ray of dorsal fin long and threadlike. Lives in surface waters where there is very little light. Measures up to 8 feet (2.5 meters) long. Found from Virginia to Brazil.

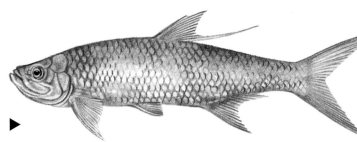

ALBULIDAE FAMILY

Bonefish

Albula vulpes

Tapered body; pointed nose; well-developed, down-turned mouth. Last ray on dorsal and anal fins is filament-shaped. Tends to come into the coastal sandy beds with the tide. Found on coral sea beds with abundant sandy areas and reef channels. Grows over 3 feet (1 meter) long. Found from New Brunswick to Brazil.

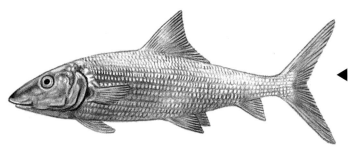

ATHERINIDAE FAMILY

Hardhead silverside

Atherinimorus stipes

Small fish that form schools of hundreds of individuals. Shiny bodies particularly striking in the light of the camera flash or flashlight beam. Live near caves and shady areas and feed on plankton. Many fish, including tarpon, prefer them as prey. Grow to 4 inches (10 centimeters) long. Found from Florida to Brazil.

SYNODONTIDAE FAMILY

Sand diver

Synodus intermedius

Robust, elongated body, flattened ventrally. Wide mouth, showing small but numerous teeth. Dark spot on the operculum and a series of yellowish longitudinal stripes on its flanks. Lives on sandy sea floors, where it buries itself. Grows up to 20 inches (55 centimeters) long. Found from North Carolina to Brazil.

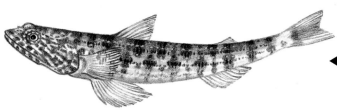

ANTENNARIDAE FAMILY

Longlure frogfish
Antennarius multiocellatus

Deep, spherical body; stubby pelvic and pectoral fins; high dorsal fin with long filament for luring prey. Camouflaged to darken when frightened; motionless unless closely approached. Up to 5.5 inches (14 centimeters) long. Found from Florida to the Caribbean.

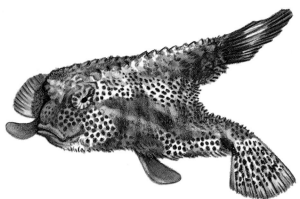

HOLOCENTRIDAE FAMILY

Longspine squirrelfish
Holocentrus rufus

Compressed, oval body; front of dorsal fin has robust white-tipped spiny rays. During the day it hides in crevices; at night it hunts for mollusks, crustaceans, and echinoderms. Up to 11 inches (28 centimeters) long. Found from Bermuda to Venezuela.

OGCOCEPHALIDAE FAMILY

Spotted batfish
Ogcocephalus radiatus

Strangely shaped, like a flattened disc with stubby pectoral fins and a tail. Its back is covered with small dark spots. It likes both rocky and sandy beds, tending to bury itself in the latter. Measures up to 15 inches (38 centimeters) long. Found in Florida and in the Bahamas.

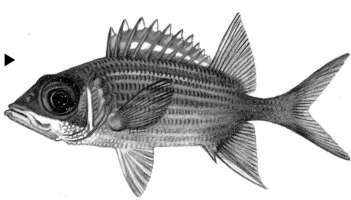

Blackbar soldierfish
Myripristis jacobus

Oval-bodied; big head; large eyes. Red body with a black bar covering the rear edge of the opercula. Stays hidden in caves in the daytime; swims upside-down because of the light that reflects off the sea bed. Measures up to 8 inches (20 centimeters) long. Found from Georgia to Brazil right to the Cape Verde Islands.

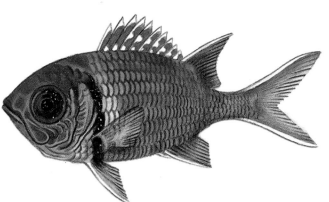

FISTULARIDAE FAMILY

Bluespotted cornetfish
Fistularia tabacaria

Elongated body; tubular nose; terminal mouth. Two central rays are elongated. Found near underwater meadows and reefs with sandy beds, alone or in small groups. Up to 6 feet (almost 2 meters) long. Found from Nova Scotia to Brazil.

AULOSTOMATIDAE FAMILY

Trumpetfish
Aulostomus maculatus

Elongated body; tubular nose; terminal mouth with a thin barbel underneath its lower jaw. The dorsal fin consists of a series of separate spiny rays. Lives close to reefs where it camouflages itself by changing color and swimming in an almost vertical position. Timid and hard to approach. Can measure over 3 feet (1 meter) long. Found from Florida to Brazil.

SYNGNATHIDAE FAMILY

Lined seahorse

Hippocampus erectus

Unique body shape, made up of bony rings on which its head is set at an angle. Found in areas rich in vegetation, where it camouflages itself by anchoring to the algae with its prehensile tail. Grows up to 6.5 inches (17 centimeters) long. Found from Nova Scotia to Argentina.

SCORPAENIDAE FAMILY

Spotted scorpionfish

Scorpaena plumieri

Powerful body; growths and appendages on nose. Greenish brown with red shading. Three dark vertical bars on the tail. The inside of the pectoral fins is dark with small white marks. This is one of the most common scorpionfish on coral reefs. Grows up to 16 inches (40 centimeters) long. Found from New York to Brazil.

DACTYLOPTERIDAE FAMILY

Flying gurnard

Dactylopterus volitans

Tapered body; stubby head flattened at the back. Distinctively large pectoral fins, which have beautiful blue spots and stripes when distended. The initial rays of the ventral fins are free and mobile, so that the fish can almost walk on the sea floor. Lives on sandy or detrital sea beds and among algae. Despite its name and its large fins, it is not a flying fish. Grows up to 18 inches (45 centimeters) long. Found along a large part of the Atlantic coast.

SERRANIDAE FAMILY

Jewfish

Epinephelus itajara

One of the biggest Atlantic groupers. Wide, flat head. Greenish gray in color with small black marks. Usually makes its den in caves or wrecks. Grows up to 8 feet (2.5 meters) long. Its sheer size makes it potentially dangerous. Found from Florida to Brazil and in Africa from Senegal to Congo.

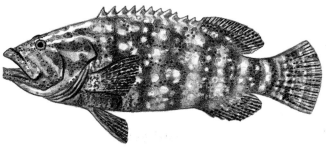

Marbled grouper

Dermatolepis inermis or *Epinephelus inermis*

A rather large grouper; wide body and large head, with a concave dorsal profile. The snout is more pointed than in the other species of its family. It is rather shy and tends to stay hidden within caves along the deeper walls of the reef, living at depths of up to 656 feet (200 meters). Younger individuals are brown with white spots; adults are yellowish with small dark and white spots. Grows up to 36 inches (91 centimeters) long. Found from Florida to Brazil.

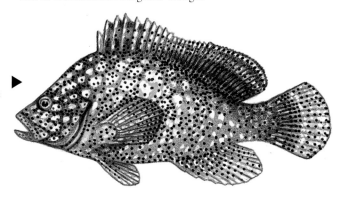

Nassau grouper
Ephinephelus striatus

Tapered body; small pelvic fins. Common on coral sea beds, where it rarely strays from the area immediately surrounding its den. Changes color rapidly when frightened or curious. Shoals of thousands form in small areas for spawning. Grows over 3 feet (1 meter) long. Widespread from North Carolina to Brazil.

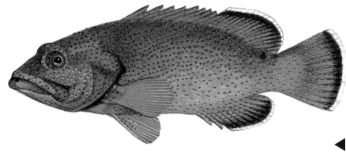

Red hind
Epinephelus guttatus

One of the most common groupers in shallow coral sea beds; often seen resting immobile on the bottom. Light-colored body with reddish marks. Dorsal, anal, and caudal fins have black edges. Measures up to 24 inches (60 centimeters) long. Found from Florida to Brazil.

Graysby
Epinephelus cruentatus

Grouper with a small, tapered body; rounded edge to its tail. Light-colored body with numerous reddish marks all over. Lives on coral beds from the surface to depths of 230 feet (70 meters). Grows up to 12 inches (30 centimeters) long. Found from Florida to Brazil.

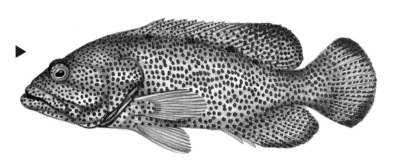

Coney
Epinephelus fulvus

Tapered body; straight-edged or slightly rounded caudal fin with distinct corners. Coloring tends to differ with depth. Gregarious; prefers reefs abounding in crevices, from which it does not often stray. Allows divers to approach slowly. Grows up to 16 inches (40 centimeters) long. Found from Florida to Brazil.

Tiger grouper
Mycteroperca tigris

Tapered body; distinctive, light-colored vertical bars on its sides, which contribute to its tigerish looks. Background color tends to red. Young fish are yellow. Lives in sheltered parts of the reef. Measures up to 33 inches (85 centimeters) long. Found from Florida to Brazil.

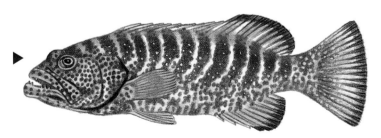

Sand perch
Diplectrum formosum

Small, elongated, slightly compressed body. Pre-operculum has two groups of diverging spines. Light-colored with blue horizontal stripes on its head and sides. Lives in meadowlands or coral, where it digs dens for itself. Measures up to 10 inches (25 centimeters) long. Found from North Carolina to Uruguay.

Greater soapfish

Rypticus saponaceus

Pointed front profile; flattened on the back of the head. Dorsal fin set back with a rounded rear edge. Lives in shallow water close to reefs and on sandy beds. If startled, secretes a mucus poisonous to other fish. Measures up to 13 inches (33 centimeters) long. Found from Florida to Brazil and in the eastern Atlantic.

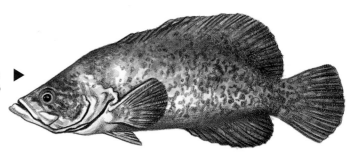

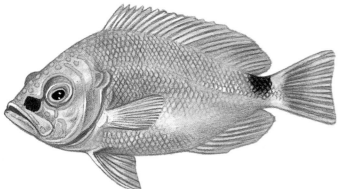

Butter hamlet

Hypoplectrus unicolor

Deep, compressed body. Lower edge of the pre-operculum finely toothed. Distinct, saddle-shaped mark on caudal peduncle. Prefers coral reefs, where it swims close to the sea bed. Measures up to 5 inches (13 centimeters) long. Found from Florida to Brazil.

Barred hamlet

Hypoplectrus puella

Compressed body; slightly pointed snout. Brown-yellow with a dark triangular blotch in the center of each flank. Prefers rocky, shallow waters and coral reefs up to depths of 75 feet (23 meters). Can be approached, but is quick to flee into crevices for shelter. Measures up to 5 inches (13 centimeters) long. Found from Florida to the Caribbean.

Indigo hamlet

Hypoplectrus indigo

Similar to barred hamlet, but distinguished by its bluish color with vertical white bars. Prefers coral sea beds, where it swims close to the bottom. Can be approached slowly. Measures up to 5 inches (13 centimeters) long. Found from Florida to the Caymans to Belize.

Tobaccofish

Serranus tabacarius

Tapered body; broad horizontal stripe of brownish orange. Lives close to the sea bed on the border between reefs and sandy beds or in areas strewn with reef detritus. Tends to become gregarious at depths greater than 165 feet (50 meters). Measures up to 7 inches (18 centimeters) long. Found from Florida to Brazil.

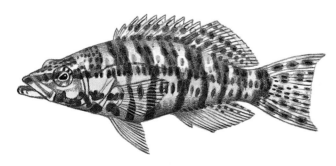

Tigerfish

Serranus tigrinus

Small, elongated, compressed body; pointed snout. Opercula spiny with toothed edges. Marked with dark vertical bars. Tips of caudal lobes yellowish. Lives on coral sea beds or meadowlands. Measures up to 6 inches (15 centimeters) long. Common in the Caribbean.

Peppermint bass

Liopropoma rubre

Small, tapered body; double dorsal fin. Tip of dorsal, anal, and tail fins are the same color. Flanks have red stripes. Tends to stay hidden in crevices and hollows and is not often seen, although it is common. Measures over 3 inches (8 centimeters) long. Found from Florida to Venezuela.

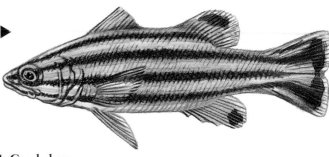

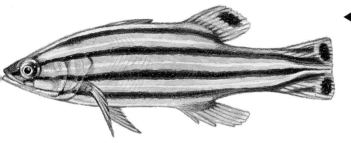

GRAMMATIDAE FAMILY

Fairy basslet

Gramma loreto

Small with highly characteristic coloring: half purple, half yellow. Lives in small schools in hollows and crevices, where it swims upside-down because of the reflected light. Measures over 3 inches (8 centimeters) long. Found from Bermuda to Venezuela.

Candy bass

Liopropoma carnabi

Small with tapered body and double dorsal fin. The second dorsal fin is characterized by a black spot edged in blue, which also appears on both lobes of the caudal fin. Lives in dark crevices in the reef at depths of between 50 and 230 feet (15 and 70 meters). Grows up to 2.5 inches (6 centimeters) long. Found from Florida to the Antilles.

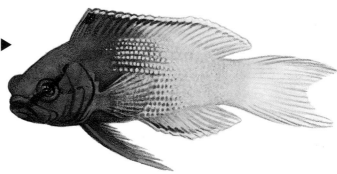

APOGONIDAE FAMILY

Spotted cardinalfish

Apogon maculatus

Small, robust, oval body; deep caudal peduncle. Red with a spot on the operculum and at base of second dorsal fin. Prefers surface water, caves during the day. Measures over 5 inches (13 centimeters) long. Found from Florida to the Gulf of Mexico.

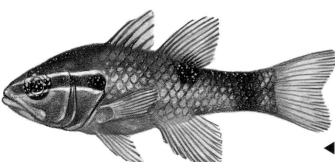

Mimic cardinal fish

Apogon phenax

Small with an oval, robust body and well-developed caudal peduncle. Pink in color with a red band at the base of the second dorsal fin and the anal fin. The caudal peduncle has two vertical black stripes. Prefers coralline and rocky sea beds with sandy areas, from 10 to 165 feet (3 to 50 meters) in depth, where it takes shelter in caves during the day. Grows up to 3 inches (7.5 centimeters) long. Found from Florida to Venezuela.

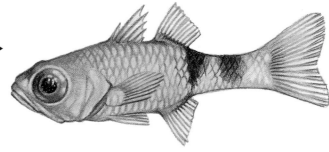

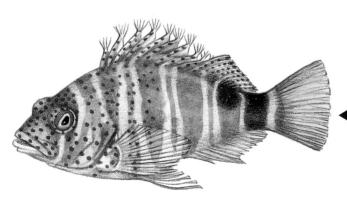

CIRRHITIDAE FAMILY

Redspotted hawkfish

Amblycirrhitus pinos

Small, deep body; pointed nose. Spiny rays of dorsal fin have fringed points. Distinctive red spots on nose, back, and dorsal fin. Lives on reefs, where it waits in ambush on the sea bed. Measures over 4 inches (11 centimeters) long. Found from Florida to the Gulf of Mexico.

PRIACANTHIDAE FAMILY

Glasseye snapper
Priacanthus cruentatus

▶

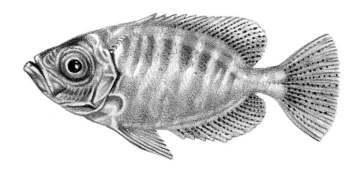

Robust, compressed body; square head; oblique mouth angled upward; very large eyes. Reddish with silvery bars that disappear on the back. Prefers surface waters, where it inhabits the less illuminated areas during the day. Measures up to 12 inches (30 centimeters) long. Found in circumtropical waters.

CENTROPOMIDAE FAMILY

Snook
Centropomus undecimalis

Robust body; pointed head; dorsal fin has a sharply angled profile. The lateral line is dark and continues to the rear edge of the tail. Lives in mangrove-filled coastal waters. Measures over 4 feet (over 1 meter) long. Found from South Carolina to Brazil.

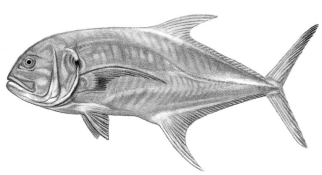

Bar jack
Caranx ruber

Elongated, tapering, silvery body, marked at the base of the dorsal fin by a dark band that stretches to the lower caudal lobe. Lives in shoals of varying size and often follows shoals of mullet and stingrays to feed on invertebrates they uncover. Measures up to 24 inches (60 centimeters) long. Found from New Jersey to Venezuela.

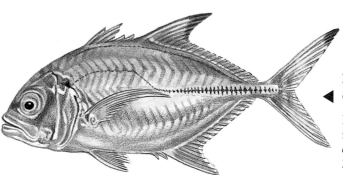

MALACANTHIDAE FAMILY

◀ ### Sand tilefish
Malacanthus plumieri

Elongated body; very large lips; crescent-shaped tail with pointed lobes. Yellowish blue with yellow and blue stripes on the head. Tail is often yellow. Lives on sandy and rubble-strewn sea beds, where it digs a den. Measures up to 24 inches (60 centimeters) long. Found from North Carolina to Brazil.

▶

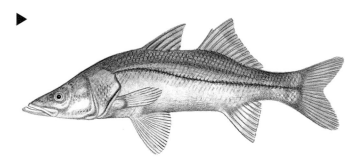

CARANGIDAE FAMILY

◀ ### Crevalle jack
Caranx hippos

Deep, elongated body, very tapered and convex at the front. Thin, characteristically forked tail. Young are gregarious and more common in coastal waters; adults tend to be solitary, more common in open water and along the outer edge of the reef. Measures over 3 feet (1 meter) long. Found from Nova Scotia to Uruguay and in the eastern Atlantic.

▶

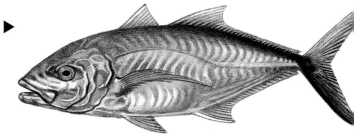

Horse-eye jack
◀ *Caranx latus*

Relatively deep, compressed body. Its yellow tail distinguishes it from the other carangids. Lives in shoals in open water above the deepest reefs, often mixing with other carangids. Measures up to 28 inches (70 centimeters) long. Found from New Jersey to Brazil.

Palometa
Trachinotus goodei

Lozenge-shaped body, distinguished by large rays on the dorsal and anal fins. Silver color with 3 to 5 vertical black streaks. Lives in coastal waters among coral formations. Measures up to 20 inches (50 centimeters) long. Found from Massachusetts to Argentina.

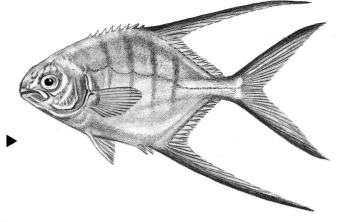

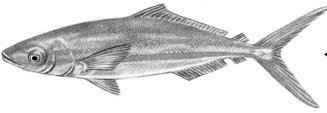

Rainbow fish
Elagatis bipinnulata

Elongated, spindle-shaped body with 2 light blue horizontal stripes separated by a green or yellowish streak. Common in open water; often moves in close to the outer slopes of the reef. Lives in shoals and seems to be attracted by the air bubbles produced by scuba-diving equipment. Measures up to 4 feet (over 1 meter) long. Found in all circumtropical waters.

Yellow jack
Caranx bartholomaei

Medium-sized carangid with tapered, compressed, but not extremely elevated body; large eyes. Light blue in color with silvery tones on its body; yellow fins. Adults often have a black spot on the apex of the opercula. Mostly solitary or may live in small groups along the outer reefs between the surface and 165 feet (50 meters). Grows up to 35 inches (90 centimeters) long. Found from Massachusetts to Brazil.

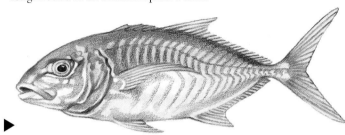

Black jack
Caranx lugubris

Medium-sized jack with tapered, compressed body; head has inclined dorsal profile. Dorsal and anal fins long and symmetrical. Grayish in color, more or less dark, with an almost black tail and fins, a distinctive characteristic of the species. Mostly solitary or may live in pairs in open waters, sometimes near steep slopes to depths of over 984 feet (300 meters). Grows up to 39 inches (100 centimeters) long. Found from Florida to Brazil.

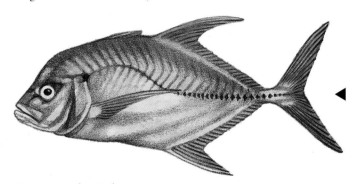

Greater amberjack
Seriola dumerili

Elongated, slightly compressed body; small eyes; slightly rounded snout. Second dorsal fin less wide than in other carangids, but extends across most of the back. The surface of its body is smooth, with no bony shields. It is bronze-colored with a dark oblique band that covers the eyes. An amber band runs along the flanks. Lives in large schools that often frequent coastal waters to depths of more than 140 feet (43 meters). Grows to more than 5 feet (150 centimeters) long. Found throughout the temperate Atlantic.

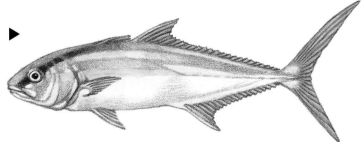

LUTJANIDAE FAMILY

Yellowtail snapper
Ocyurus chrysurus

Elongated body; pronounced forked tail with pointed lobes. Purple-blue color with horizontal yellow stripe and small spots. Swims alone or in small groups close to reef or meadowlands. More active at night. Measures up to 30 inches (75 centimeters) long. Found from Massachusetts to Brazil.

Mutton snapper
Lutjanus analis

Robust, deep body; olive-colored with blackish streaks that are more marked in fish under 16 inches (40 centimeters) long. Adults prefer rocky and coral sea beds; young found more often on sandy beds and in meadowlands. Measures up to 30 inches (75 centimeters) long. Found from Massachusetts to Brazil.

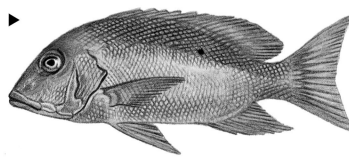

Schoolmaster
Lutjanus apodus

Robust body, slightly compressed; pointed head and well-developed mouth. Color varies from silvery to bronze. Characteristic yellow fins and blue stripes on the snout. Lives in groups of a few dozen individuals, which usually remain a short distance from the sea floor in areas with abundant gorgonians and large corals, at depths of between 6.5 and 98 feet (2 and 30 meters). Grows up to 24 inches (60 centimeters) long. Found throughout the Caribbean and along the temperate coasts of the American continent.

Gray snapper
Lutjanus griseus

Robust, slightly compressed body; pointed head and well-developed mouth. Color varies from more or less dark gray to reddish. No particularly distinctive features except for a dark band, not always visible, that masks the eyes and extends from the mouth to the beginning of the dorsal fin. Lives in small schools that commonly frequent coastal waters and mangrove forests as well as reefs, from the surface to 82 feet (25 meters). Grows up to 24 inches (60 centimeters) long. Found from Massachusetts to Brazil.

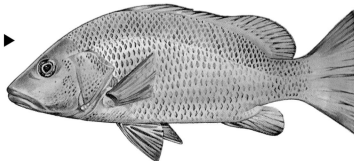

HAEMULIDAE FAMILY

Porkfish
Anisotremus virginicus

Compressed body, very deep at the front. Two characteristic dark vertical bars on the head and a series of blue and yellow horizontal streaks. Swims alone or in small groups, more common above the reef during the day. Young act as cleaner fish. Measures up to 16 inches (40 centimeters) long. Found from Florida to Brazil.

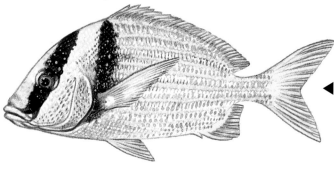

Bluestriped grunt
Haemulon sciurus

Deep, compressed body, with dark-colored rear part, including the dorsal and tail fins. Background color is yellow with numerous blue horizontal stripes. Forms large shoals near the coast on rocky or sandy beds. Measures up to 18 inches (45 centimeters) long. Found from South Carolina to Brazil.

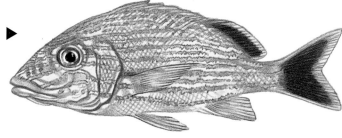

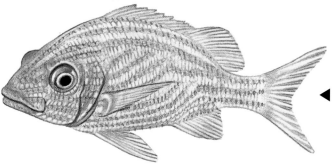

French grunt
Haemulon flavolineatum

Deep body; pointed snout; small mouth. Yellowish with numerous blue streaks, horizontal above the lateral line and oblique below. Prefers coral sea beds, where it forms shoals of up to 1,000 fish. Likes poorly illuminated areas. Measures up to 12 inches (30 centimeters) long. Found from South Carolina to Brazil.

Smallmouth grunt

Haemulon chrysargyreum

Tapered, slightly compressed body; small head and large eyes. Silvery white in color, with 5 to 6 horizontal yellow stripes on its flanks; yellow fins. Lives in schools near the sea floor in proximity to large coral formations on reefs between 6.5 and 60 feet (2 and 18 meters) deep, where wave action is more pronounced. Grows up to 9 inches (23 centimeters) long. Found from Florida to Brazil.

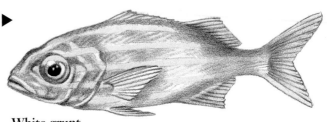

Black grunt

Haemulon bonariense

Compressed body with rounded dorsal profile; short snout and fairly large eyes. Well-developed dorsal fin. Its basic color is silvery gray, with dark spots in the center of the scales, which are arranged in oblique lines. The caudal fin is black. Lives in small schools, sometimes mingling with other grunts. Lives in different habitats, including meadows of phanerogams, sandy areas, and coral reefs at depths of between 10 and 66 feet (3 and 20 meters). Grows up to 12 inches (30 centimeters) long. Found from the Caribbean to Brazil.

White grunt

Haemulon plumieri

Tapered, fairly wide body with robust head and slightly concave dorsal profile. Bluish silver or yellow in color, with blue stripes on the head only. Lives in large schools near the sea floor close to large colonies of acropora corals on reefs from 6.5 to 128 feet (2 to 39 meters) deep. Sometimes two individuals may demonstrate territorial behavior by swimming mouth to mouth. Grows up to 18 inches (45 centimeters) long. Found from Maryland to Brazil.

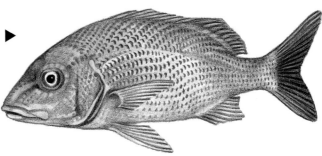

Spanish grunt

Haemulon macrostomum

Compressed body slightly more stubby than most other grunts. Can be recognized by the horizontal dark stripes on the upper portion of the flanks and the profile of its yellow back. The fins are dark and edged with yellow. It is mostly solitary, but sometimes mingles with schools of other grunts, in which it stands out due to its color. Frequents sheltered areas of the reef between 16 and 66 feet (5 and 20 meters) deep. Grows up to 17 inches (43 centimeters) long. Found from Massachusetts to Brazil.

White margate

Haemulon album

Compressed body with wide upper profile. Grayish color sometimes interrupted by three dark stripes on the flanks. Blackish caudal fin. Lives in extremely varied environments: phanerogam meadows, sandy sea beds, and coral reefs at depths of from 6.5 to 60 feet (2 to 18 meters). Lives isolated in small groups. Measures up to 24 inches (60 centimeters) long and is the largest of the Caribbean grunts. Found from Florida to Brazil.

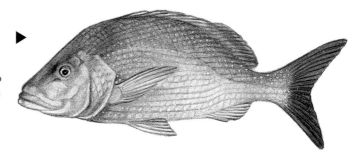

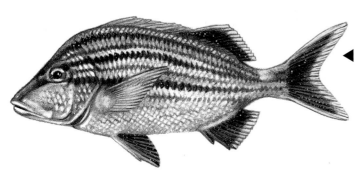

SCIAENIDAE FAMILY

Reef croaker

Odontoscion dentex

Elongated, compressed body; big, oblique, terminal mouth. Reddish body with a black blotch at the base of the pelvic fin. Prefers rocky habitats and shallow coral reefs, tending to stay in poorly lit areas. Measures up to 10 inches (25 centimeters) long. Found from Florida to Brazil.

Jack-knife fish
Equetus lanceolatus

Body deep in front and very pointed in rear. Characteristically deep forward dorsal fin, especially in the young. Dark bar runs from the tip of the dorsal fin to the tail. Prefers the darker parts of reefs and hollows. Measures up to 10 inches (25 centimeters) long. Found from South Carolina to Brazil.

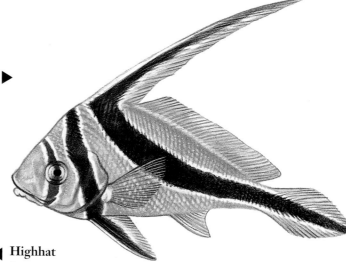

Highhat
Pareques acuminatus

Body wide yet stubby in the anterior portion, with an evident dorsal fin that is nevertheless not very wide. It is reddish brown with whitish longitudinal stripes. Prefers surface waters near rocky and coralline sea beds near caves and poorly illuminated areas. Up to 9 inches (23 centimeters) long. Common from South Carolina to Brazil.

Spotted drum
Equetus punctatus

Small, compressed body; well-developed head and tapered posterior portion. The very wide, falcate initial rays of the dorsal fin are characteristic. The caudal fin is lozenge-shaped. Its basic coloring is white, with wide dark bands oblique on the head, becoming horizontal along the flanks. The second half of the dorsal, caudal, and anal fins are dark and spotted with white. Mostly solitary, living on coralline sea beds at depths of between 10 and 98 feet (3 and 30 meters), sheltered in caves. It is nocturnal. Grows up to 10 inches (25 centimeters) long. Found from Florida to Brazil.

MULLIDAE FAMILY

Yellow goatfish
Mulloidichthys martinicus

Tapered body; snout has a slightly convex and pointed edge. Olive-colored back with light-colored flanks; horizontal yellow bar stretching to the tail. Forms small shoals on the sandy beds close to reefs. Measures up to 16 inches (40 centimeters) long. Found from the Caribbean to the Cape Verde Islands.

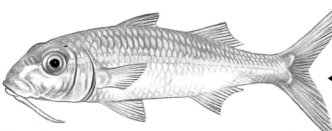

Spotted goatfish
Pseudopeneus maculatus

Tapered body; slightly pointed snout. Edge of operculum has a spine, quite pronounced in some cases. Three large blackish blotches on the sides of the body. Forms small groups of 4 to 5 to hunt. Grows over 10 inches (26 centimeters) long. Found from Florida to Brazil.

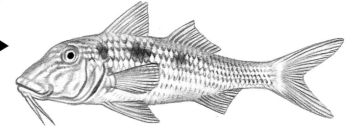

PEMPHERIDAE FAMILY

Glassfish
Pempheris schomburgki

Small, compressed, oval body; tapered at the rear. Silvery-pink color, with long black-edged anal fin. Lives in shoals in grottoes or reef crevices, coming out at night. Measures up to 6 inches (16 centimeters) long. Found from Florida to Brazil.

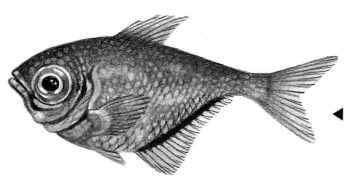

KYPHOSIDAE FAMILY

Bermuda chub
Kyphosus sectatrix

Deep, oval body; small terminal mouth. Gray color with thin bronze horizontal stripes. Forms shoals close to coral and rocky sea beds rich in algae. Up to 30 inches (76 centimeters) long. Found from Massachusetts to Brazil.

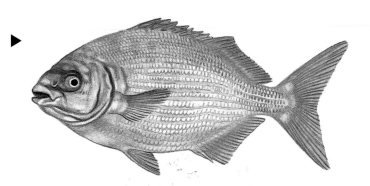

CHAETODONTIDAE FAMILY

Foureye butterflyfish
Chaetodon capistratus

Deep, compressed body; yellow fins with small black spot on rear edge of the dorsal fin. Tends to become dark at night. Usually swims in pairs close to reefs and rocky sea beds. Grows up to 8 inches (20 centimeters) long. Found from Massachusetts to Brazil.

EPHIPPIDAE FAMILY

Atlantic spadefish
Chaetodipterus faber

Very deep, compressed body; lobes of dorsal and anal fins very elongated at the rear. Grayish with 4 to 5 dark vertical bands. Forms small schools that swim in open water away from the reef. Sometimes spontaneously approaches divers. Grows up to 36 inches (90 centimeters) long. Found from Massachusetts to Brazil.

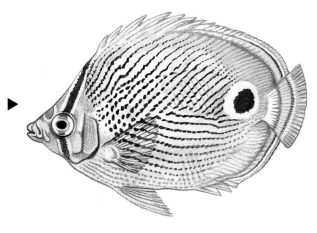

Reef butterflyfish
Chaetodon sedentarius

Deep, compressed body; almost vertical rear profile. Yellowish coloring with a dark, wide band at the rear, running from dorsal to anal fin. Prefers coral bottoms where it goes as deep as 295 feet (90 meters). Measures up to 6 inches (15 centimeters) long. Found from North Carolina to Brazil.

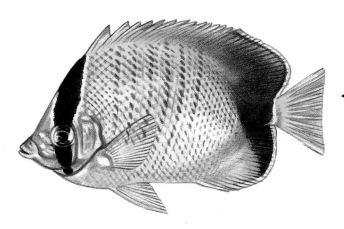

Spotfin butterflyfish
Chaetodon ocellatus

Deep, compressed body; yellow fins; small black mark on rear edge of dorsal fin. Tends to turn a darker color at night. Generally swims in pairs close to reefs and rocky bottoms. Grows up to 8 inches (20 centimeters) long. Found from Massachusetts to Brazil.

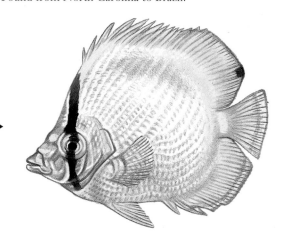

Longsnout butterflyfish

Chaetodon aculeatus

Compressed, very deep body; well-developed spiny rays on dorsal fin; long, pointed snout. Solitary; prefers the deepest coral sea beds and reef crevices, where it takes shelter when frightened. Measures up to 4 inches (10 centimeters) long. Found from Florida to Venezuela.

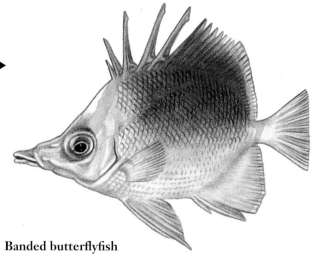

POMACANTHIDAE FAMILY

Gray angelfish

Pomacanthus arcuatus

Deep, compressed body; dorsal and caudal lobes pointed at rear; tail fin has a straight trailing edge. Gray-brown coloring, with a very pale mouth. Lives alone or in pairs in the richest areas of the reef. Measures up to 20 inches (50 centimeters) long. Found from Bermuda to Brazil.

Banded butterflyfish

Chaetodon striatus

Deep, compressed body; whitish coloring with 3 dark slanting bars, the first of which covers the eye. Young fish have an ocellar marking on the caudal peduncle. Lives alone or in pairs, close to coral. Measures up to 6 inches (16 centimeters) long. Found from Massachusetts to Brazil.

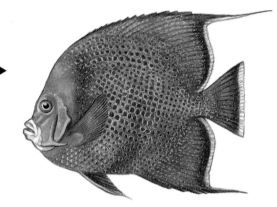

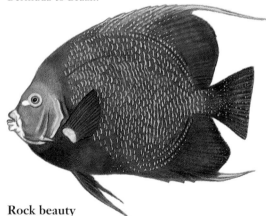

Rock beauty

Holacanthus tricolor

Distinctive colors: yellow front body and tail sections, black central section, and blue mouth. Pointed lobes to dorsal, anal, and caudal fins. Extremely territorial; stays close to its own area of the reef. Measures up to 8 inches (20 centimeters) long. Found from Georgia to Brazil.

French angelfish

Pomacanthus paru

Rounded, compressed body; rear lobes of dorsal and anal fins very pointed. Blackish coloring with yellow markings on snout and pectoral fins. Prefers the reef closest to the surface and richest in gorgonians. Measures up to 12 inches (30 centimeters) long. Found from Florida to Brazil.

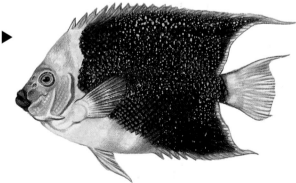

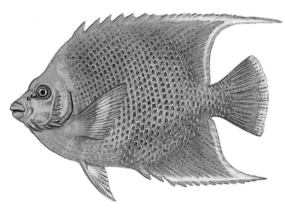

Blue angelfish

Holacanthus bermudensis

Deep, compressed body; rear lobes of dorsal and anal fins very pointed, extending past the trailing edge of the caudal fin. Blue with yellow-edged fins. Prefers the reef closest to the surface. Measures up to 15 inches (38 centimeters) long. Found from Florida to Yucatan.

Queen angelfish
Holacanthus ciliaris

Deep, compressed body; rear lobes of dorsal and anal fins very pointed, extending past the trailing caudal fin. Yellow, densely spotted with blue on the sides and a blue blotch on the head. Lives on the reef closest to the surface and also in the deepest parts at over 165 feet (50 meters). Measures up to 18 inches (45 centimeters) long. Found from Bermuda to Brazil.

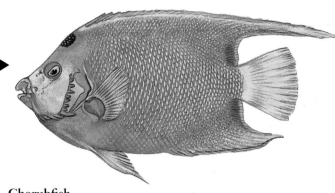

Cherubfish
Centropyge argi

Small, oval body. Yellow markings on head and part of the back; blue sides, belly, and tail. Prefers the deepest parts of the coral bed, usually over 98 feet (30 meters), where it sometimes forms small groups. Measures up to 3 inches (8 centimeters) long. Found from Bermuda to Venezuela.

POMACENTRIDAE FAMILY

Blue chromis
Chromis cyanea

Small, oval body; deeply cleft tail fin. Bluish with black-edged caudal lobes. Quite common around the reef, where it forms shoals. Measures up to 5 inches (13 centimeters) long. Found from Florida to Venezuela.

Brown chromis
Chromis multilineata

Gray, swarthy-colored fish with a black spot at the base of the pectoral fins and yellow tips to the dorsal fin and caudal lobes. Lives in groups above coral formations. Measures up to 6.5 inches (17 centimeters) long. Found from Florida to Brazil.

Beaugregory
Stegastes leucostictos

Small, slightly oval in shape; forked tail with rounded lobes. Brownish coloring with a light yellow tail. Territorial; prefers sandy sea beds rich in algae and detritus. Measures up to 4 inches (10 centimeters) long. Found from Maine to Brazil.

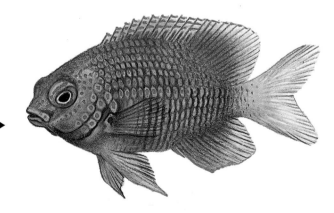

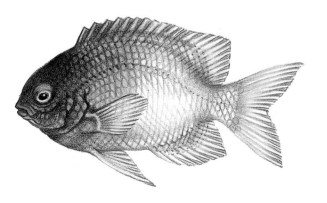

Bicolor damselfish
Stegastes partitus

Small, compressed, oval body; small terminal mouth. Dark front section; white at the back. Lives close to the higher parts of the reef, where it defends its territory from other fishes of the same species. Measures up to 5 inches (12 centimeters) long. Found from Florida to the Gulf of Mexico.

Three-spot damselfish

Stegastes planifrons

Small, compressed, oval body; small terminal mouth. Dark coloring with yellow-rimmed eyes and black spots at the base of pectoral fins and caudal peduncle. Lives in the reef closest to the surface, rich in algae, where it establishes its own territory and defends it tenaciously. Measures up to 5 inches (12 centimeters) long. Found from Florida to the Gulf of Mexico.

Sergeant major

Abudefduf saxatilis

Compressed, ovoid, deep body; covered with rough scales, which extend to the fins. Silvery white with dark vertical bars and a yellow stripe at the base of the dorsal fin. Lives in shoals in the reef closest to the surface. Measures up to 8 inches (20 centimeters) long. Found from Rhode Island to Uruguay.

Yellowtail damselfish

Microspatodon chrysurus

Small, robust body. Brownish coloring with small blue markings and distinctive yellow tail. The young tend to stay among the branches of fire corals, sometimes acting as cleaner fish. Adults occupy small territories in the reef closest to the surface. Measures up to 8 inches (20 centimeters) long. Found from Florida to Venezuela.

Cocoa damselfish

Stegastes variabilis

Oval body with pointed snout and slightly indented caudal fin. Well-developed dorsal fin. Olive brown on the back; tends to become yellowish on the belly. Young individuals are blue in the dorsal area, with a black spot on the dorsal fin and one on the caudal peduncle. Lives near coral reefs between the surface and a depth of 98 feet (30 meters). Establishes territories on the sea bed, which it fiercely defends, especially during the mating season. Grows up to 5 inches (12.5 centimeters) long. Found from Florida to Brazil.

LABRIDAE FAMILY

Spanish hogfish

Bodianus rufus

Robust body; pointed head. Purple back; rest of the body yellowish. Swims continuously close to the sea bed, showing no fear at all, not even of divers. Measures up to 16 inches (40 centimeters) long. Found from Florida to Brazil.

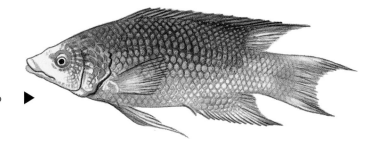

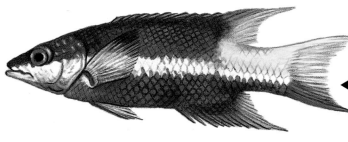

Spotfin hogfish

Bodianus pulchellus

Robust body; pointed snout; pointed rear lobes on dorsal and anal fins. Adults are red with yellow tail and partially yellow caudal fin. Common on coral reefs over 65 feet (20 meters) deep. Measures up to 8 inches (20 centimeters) long. Found from Florida to Brazil.

Creole wrasse
Clepticus parrae

Large, tapered body; pointed lobes of dorsal and anal fins; slightly lunar-shaped tail. Adults are dark purple with a yellowish rear part and a pale mouth. Prefers the deepest parts of the reef, where it forms large shoals before sunset. Measures up to 12 inches (30 centimeters) long. Found from North Carolina to the Gulf of Mexico.

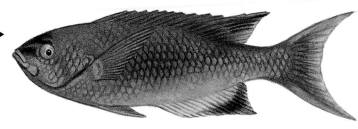

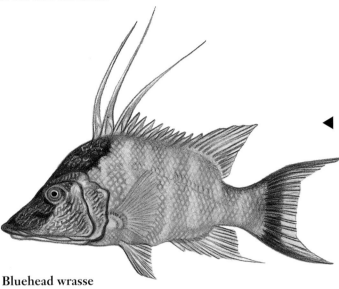

Hogfish
Lachnolaimus maximus

Fairly large; pointed head. Identified by the very well developed first rays of dorsal fin. Whitish coloring with a dark bar stretching along the back from mouth to tail. Prefers sandy sea beds, where it likes to dig for its prey. Measures up to 35 inches (90 centimeters) long. Found from North Carolina to Brazil.

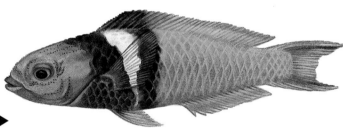

Bluehead wrasse
Thalassoma bifasciatum

Elongated, compressed body. Coloring varies greatly according to age. Adults are greenish at the rear and bluish at the front with black and white stripes in between. The young are yellowish. Found in a great number of different habitats. Measures up to 7 inches (18 centimeters) long. Found from Florida to Venezuela.

Puddingwife
Halichoeres radiatus

Very deep body. Blue-green coloring with yellow-edged caudal fin. Uncommon and hard to approach: swims continuously and is very suspicious. Measures up to 20 inches (50 centimeters) long. Found from North Carolina to Brazil.

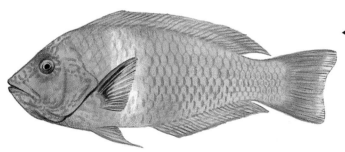

Slippery dick
Halichoeres bivittatus

Deep, tapered body; large caudal fin. Extremely variable coloring, mainly greenish with a horizontal dark band along the sides. Lobes of caudal fin have dark tips. Found in various different habitats, from coral reefs to sandy sea beds to underwater meadows. Measures up to 10 inches (26 centimeters) long. Found from North Carolina to Brazil.

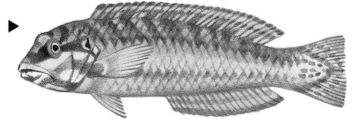

Yellowcheek wrasse
Halichoeres cyanocephalus

Robust body; blunt, rounded head. Mouth distinguished by projecting lips. Young individuals are yellow in the dorsal area, with the rest of the body blue. Adults are greenish yellow in the dorsal area, with a white belly and a wide blue band along the flanks. Lives near reefs and rocky shoals at depths of between 98 and 295 feet (30 and 90 meters). Grows up to 12 inches (30 centimeters) long. Found from Florida to Brazil.

Green razorfish

Hemipteronotus splendens

Wide, very compressed body, rounded snout, and oblique profile. Greenish in color, with a small dark lateral spot (typical of males) and eyes with a red iris. Tends to remain nearly immobile near sea beds with meadows or on sandy floors with gorgonians, at depths of between 10 and 50 feet (3 and 15 meters). If threatened, it buries itself in the sediments. Grows up to 6 inches (15 centimeters) long. Found from Florida to Brazil.

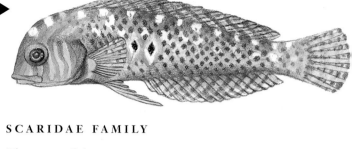

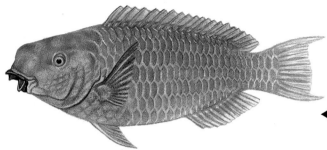

SCARIDAE FAMILY

Blue parrotfish

Scarus coeruleus

Tapered, robust body. Adult males have a characteristic frontal bump that modifies the front profile of the snout. Mainly blue in color. Feeds principally on algae and for this reason it moves swiftly from one part of the reef to another. Measures up to 35 inches (90 centimeters) long. Found from Maryland to Brazil.

Queen parrotfish

Scarus vetula

Blue-green with scales edged in pink-orange. Nose has broad blue stripes around the mouth and close to the eyes. Lives on coral reefs up to 82 feet (25 meters) deep. Measures up to 24 inches (60 centimeters) long. Found from Florida to Argentina.

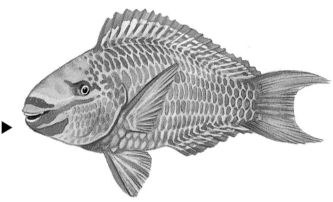

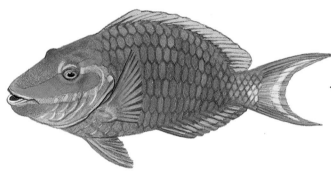

Stoplight parrotfish

Sparisoma viride

Mainly green coloring; yellow-orange slanting bars on head; caudal fin and a yellow mark on the operculum. Reasonably common where coral sea beds alternate with areas rich in algae. Measures up to 20 inches (50 centimeters) long. Found from Florida to Brazil.

Redband parrotfish

Sparisoma aurofrenatum

Green coloring with red and orange shading; orange bar at each side of the mouth; fins shaded with purple. Prefers reefs where there is an abundance of algae. Measures up to 14 inches (35 centimeters) long. Found from Florida to Brazil.

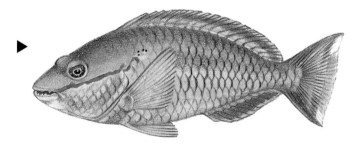

Princess parrotfish

Scarus taeniopterus

Small, greenish blue with a yellow lateral band and blue stripes on the snout. Caudal and dorsal fins have distinctively colored edges: yellow, orange, or pink. Adults live in small groups, while young and immature individuals are much more gregarious. Prefers rocky coastal areas and outer reefs, to a depth of 82 feet (25 meters). Grows up to 14 inches (35 centimeters) long. Found from Florida to Brazil.

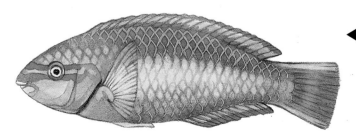

OPISTOGNATHIDAE FAMILY

Yellowhead jawfish

Opistognathus aurifrons

Small, elongated, tapered body; short, powerful head; large eyes. Blue coloring with a yellowish head. Bottom-dweller that lives close to a den it digs itself. Measures up to 4 inches (10 centimeters) long. Found from Florida to Venezuela.

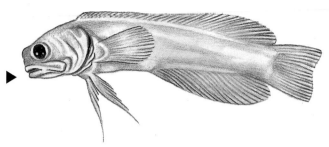

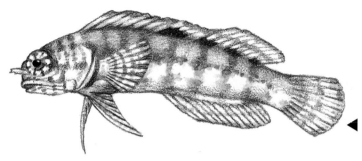

SPHYRAENIDAE FAMILY

Great barracuda

Sphyraena barracuda

Tapered, sub-cylindrical body; long, pointed snout; prominent lower jaw; 2 clearly separated dorsal fins; caudal fin slightly lunar-shaped, with pointed lobes. Coloring is silvery with dark vertical bands and small spots near the caudal fin. Lives in coastal waters above coral, sandy, or meadowland sea beds. Measures up to 6.5 feet (2 meters) long. Found in all circumtropical waters.

Mottled jawfish

Opistognathus maxillosus

Small, robust, elongated, and tapered body that ends in a short head. The square operculum is characteristic. It is whitish in color, with brownish stripes and bands on its entire body and 4 or 5 dark spots on the dorsal fin. Usually lives on detrital or sandy sea beds between 3 and 32 feet (1 and 10 meters) in depth, where it digs lairs in which it will rapidly take refuge. Grows up to 5 inches (13 centimeters) long. Found from South Carolina to the Bahamas.

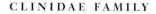

CLINIDAE FAMILY

Keys blenny

Starksia starcki

Small elongated body; wide mouth. Snout characterized by long barbels in a dorsal position. Ventral fins located in the anterior portion and are filamentous. It is light brownish yellow with darker vertical bands over its entire body. Lives at depths of between 20 and 65 feet (6 and 20 meters) on rough coralline sea beds swept by surf and currents. Grows up to 1.5 inches (4 centimeters) long. Found from Florida to the Honduras.

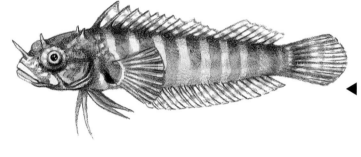

BLENNIIDAE FAMILY

Redlip blenny

Ophioblennius atlanticus

Compressed body; blunt nose; distinctive big lips. Dark with yellow or pink shading on the pectoral and caudal fins. Territorial; prefers rocky sea beds and the parts of the reef closest to the surface. Measures up to 5 inches (13 centimeters) long. Found from North Carolina to Brazil.

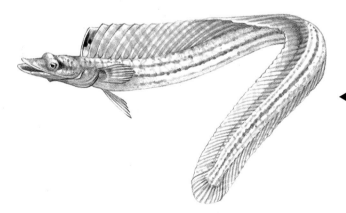

CLINIDAE FAMILY

Bluethroat pikeblenny

Chaenopsis ocellata

Long, almost serpentine body; flattened, long head similar to that of a pike. Well-developed eyes located in a dorsal position. Characteristic dorsal fin—quite wide to the front and erectile. Brownish or yellowish in color. Males have a blue throat. Lives on sandy sea beds mixed with phanerogam meadows and algae, from the surface to 10 to 13 feet (3 to 4 meters) in depth. Grows up to 5.5 inches (14 centimeters) long. Found from Florida to Cuba.

GOBIDAE FAMILY

Neon goby

Gobiosoma oceanops

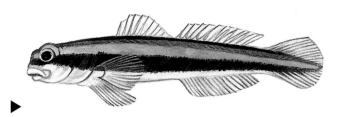

Small cleaner fish, which forms groups with others of its species in characteristic "service stations." Easily identified by its dark coloring, on which 2 blue fluorescent horizontal stripes stand out. Measures up to 2 inches (5 centimeters) long. Found from Florida to Honduras.

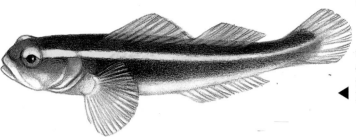

Yellowline goby

Gobiosoma horsti

Small; easily recognizable by the dark color of its back, where there is a yellow longitudinal stripe running from the eye to the tail. Usually lives between 23 and 89 feet (7 and 27 meters) in depth near sponges, where it dwells within the larger pores of tubular sponges. Grows up to 1.5 inches (4 centimeters) long. Found from Florida to the Antilles.

ACANTHURIDAE FAMILY

Surgeonfish

Acanthurus chirurgus

Deep, compressed body. Distinctive set of dark vertical bars, more or less visible. Usually lives alone or with other surgeonfish close to the reef. Measures up to 10 inches (25 centimeters) long. Found from Massachusetts to Brazil.

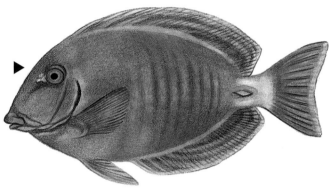

Blue tang

Acanthurus coeruleus

Similar to surgeonfish but has no vertical bars. Color can vary from powder blue to deep purple. Measures up to 12 inches (30 centimeters) long. Found from Massachusetts to Brazil.

Bahia surgeonfish

Acanthurus bahianus

Coloring varies from blue-gray to dark brown with light-colored spokes around the eyes. Prefers flat or slightly sloping coral sea beds. Measures up to 14 inches (35 centimeters) long. Found from Massachusetts to Brazil.

Gulf tang

Acanthurus randalli

May vary in color from bluish gray to dark brown. There are light-colored, radiating stripes around the eyes. Raised scales can be seen along the flanks. It prefers flat or slightly sloping coral reefs at depths of between 10 and 66 feet (3 and 20 meters). Grows up to 7 inches (18 centimeters) long. Found from Florida to the Gulf of Mexico, where it replaces the so-called ocean surgeonfish, *Acanthurus bahianus*, which is common from Massachusetts to Bermuda to Brazil.

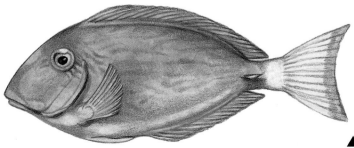

BOTHIDAE FAMILY

Peacock flounder
Bothus lunatus

Identified by the series of ocellar spots on the body and the small bluish marks on the fins. Very elongated pelvic fin that is usually erect. Lives on sandy sea beds covered in detritus, where it camouflages itself. Measures up to 16 inches (40 centimeters) long. Found from Florida to Brazil.

Queen triggerfish
Balistes vetula

Has streaming tips on dorsal and tail fins, 2 blue stripes on face, and distinctive small lines radiating from eye. Measures up to 24 inches (60 centimeters). Found in circumtropical seas.

BALISTIDAE FAMILY

Gray triggerfish
Balistes capriscus

Has small bluish spots on the back and fins. Lives alone or in small groups near rocky sea beds rich in vegetation. Particularly fond of sea urchins as food. Measures up to 12 inches (30 centimeters) long. Found from Nova Scotia to Argentina.

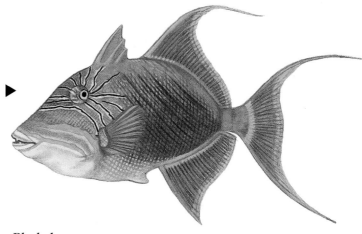

Black durgon
Melichthys niger

Blue-black body with blue stripes at the base of dorsal and anal fins. Lives in small groups along the outer reef wall at depths of up to 196 feet (60 meters). Measures up to 20 inches (50 centimeters) long. Found in circumtropical seas.

Ocean triggerfish
Canthidermis sufflamen

Oval, wide body with pointed, falcate dorsal and anal fins. Uniformly gray in color, with a black spot at the base of the pectoral fins. Solitary or lives in small groups in open waters near reefs and coral slopes at depths of between 39 and 131 feet (12 and 40 meters). During the mating season it moves to sandy sea beds. Grows up to 25.5 inches (65 centimeters) long. Found from Florida to Argentina to the Cape Verde Islands.

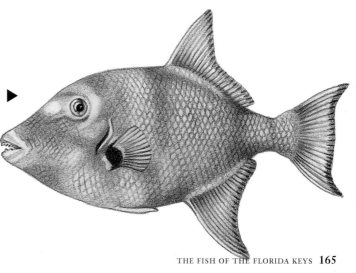

MONOCANTHIDAE FAMILY

Scrawled filefish
Aluteres scriptus

Tapered body; pointed snout; broad tail. Coloring characterized by irregular streaks and small blue markings. Solitary; lives in lagoons and along the outer reef wall, from which it heads for the open sea. Measures up to 3.5 feet (over 1 meter) long. Common in circumtropical seas.

▲

Whitespotted filefish
Cantherhines macrocerus

◀ Somewhat oval body with a ventral edge that has an evident bulge in front of the anal fin. Slightly pointed snout; more developed lower jaw. Olive gray dorsally and orange-brown ventrally; with or without white spots. Orange spines on the caudal peduncle. Lives in pairs in lagoons or near reefs with abundant gorgonians, at depths of between 16.5 and 82 feet (5 and 25 meters). Grows up to 16.5 inches (42 centimeters) long. Found from Florida to Brazil.

OSTRACIIDAE FAMILY

Smooth trunkfish
Lactophrys triqueter

Triangular silhouette; large hexagonal bony scales. Dark coloring with numerous lighter marks. Usually solitary; sometimes forms small groups. Prefers coral sea beds but can be found on sandy beds. Measures up to 12 inches (30 centimeters) long. Found from Massachusetts to Brazil.

▶

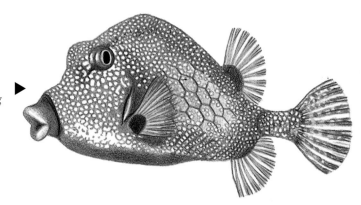

Scrawled cowfish
Lactophrys quadricornis

◀ Triangular body with long caudal peduncle and 2 spines above the eyes. Yellowish in color with numerous blue spots and stripes. Usually solitary and lives at depths of between 6 and 82 feet (2 and 25 meters), with a preference for coralline sea beds and meadows, where it camouflages itself by changing color. Grows up to 19 inches (48 centimeters) long. Found from Massachusetts to Brazil.

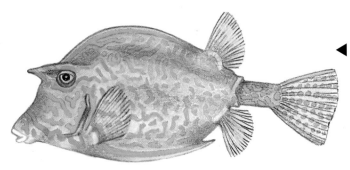

Spotted trunkfish
Lactophrys bicaudalis

Nearly polygonal body with two robust anterior spines on the anal fin. White with black spots, which appear on the fins as well. The mouth is white. It is solitary or lives in small groups at depths of between 10 and 82 feet (3 and 25 meters), on coralline sea beds mixed with sandy areas. Grows up to 18 inches (45 centimeters) long. Found from Florida to Brazil.

▶

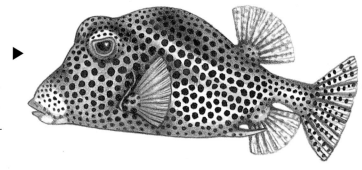

TETRAODONTIDAE FAMILY

Bandtail pufferfish
Sphoeroides spengleri

Elongated body, rounded at the front; large nostrils. Horizontal series of marks along the sides below the lateral line. Nearly always swims close to the sea bed, whether meadowlands, coral, or sandy and strewn with detritus. Measures up to 7 inches (18 centimeters) long. Found from Massachusetts to Brazil.

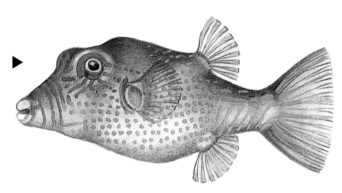

Chequered pufferfish
Sphoeroides testudineus

Round, spindle-shaped body; light geometrical lines form a grid. Prefers coastal bays, rocks, and meadowlands. Not often found close to reefs. Measures up to 12 inches (30 centimeters) long. Found from Bermuda to Brazil.

Longnose pufferfish
Canthigaster rostrata

Small; very pointed nose; small terminal mouth. Dark coloring on the back and yellowish along the sides; blue streaks and marks around the eyes, close to the mouth and on the tail. Prefers coral sea beds and meadowlands. Measures over 4 inches (11 centimeters) long. Found from Florida to Brazil.

DIODONTHIDAE FA

Burrfish
Diodon hystrix

Tapered body with a large, rounded front end; goggle eyes; mouth has a single dental plate in each jaw; skin covered in spines that become erect when the animal puffs up. Tends to stay in caves or other poorly illuminated areas of the reef during the day. Measures up to 35 inches (90 centimeters) long. Found in all circumtropical waters.

Balloonfish
Diodon holacanthus

Stubby, oval, and lightly depressed body with spines. Those on the head are rather long. If attacked, it swells, raising its spines in defense. Olive or brownish in color, with small dark spots, which are not present on the fins. Lives at depths of between 6 and 82 feet (2 and 25 meters), in lagoons, reefs with corals mixed with detrital areas, and phanerogam meadows. Grows up to 19 inches (50 centimeters) long. Found from Florida to Brazil and in many circumtropical areas.

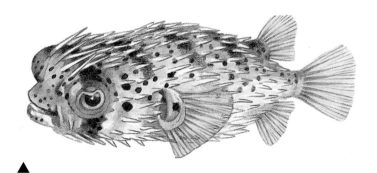

ACKNOWLEDGMENTS

The authors wish to acknowledge Ocean Divers, Captain Slate's Atlantis Dive Center, Quiescence Diving Services, Lady Cyana Divers, The Diving Site, and Southpoint Divers for their assistance in providing diving services during the research of this book. Information was also provided by the Florida Keys National Marine Sanctuary. Special thanks to Liz Johnson of WaterHouse Stock Photography for her assistance in photographic research.

PHOTOGRAPHIC CREDITS

AKG Photo: pages 10-11; **Mary Evans Picture Library:** *page 10;* **Stephen Frink/WaterHouse Stock Photography:** *pages 2-3, 7, 9, 12, 13 C, E, 14, 15 D, 16 A, B, C, 17 G, H, 18 A, B, D, 19 F, G, H, 20 A, B, 21 D, E, 22, 23, 24, 25 F, 26 A, C, D, 27 E, F, 28, 29 D, 31 E, 32 B, 33, 36 B, D, E, 37 F, G, 40 B, 44, 45, 48 A, B, D, 49, 52 A, B, C, 53 E, G, 56 A, C, 57 E, F, 60, 61, 64 C, 65 F, G, H, 68 C, 69, 72 D, 73 G, 76, 77 D, G, 80 B,C, 81 D, E, F, G, 84 A, B, D, E, 85, 88 A, B, C, D, 89 G, H, I, 92, 93 D, F, G, 96 A, 97 E, 100 A, B, 101 E, H, 104 B, C, 108 D, 112 B, C, 113 F, G, 116 A, D, 117 E, H, 120 C, D, 121 G, H, I, 124, 125 G, I, 128 A, C, 129 E, H, 132 D, E, 133 F, I, 136 B, C, D, 137 E, 140 C, D, 141 G, I;* **William Harrigan/WaterHouse Stock Photography:** *pages 1, 6, 13 D, 15 E, F, 16 D, 17 E, F, 18 C, 19 E, 21 C, 25 D, E, 26 B, 27 G, 29 E, 30, 31 C, D, 32 A, 36 A, C, 37 H, 40 A, C, D, 41, 48 C, 52 D, 53 F, 56 B, 57 D, G, H, 64 A, B, D, 65 E, 68 A, B, D, 72 A, B, C, 73 E, F, H, 77 E, F, 80A, 88 E, 89 F, 93 E, H, 96 B, C, D, 97 F, G, H, I, 100 C, D, 101 F, G, 104 A, 105, 108 A, B, 109, 112 A, D, E, 113 H, I, 116 B, C, 117 F, G, 120 A, B, 121 E, F, 125 E, F, H, 128 B, D, 129 F, G, 132 A, B, 133 G, H, 136 A, 137 F, G, 140 A, B, E, 141 F, H;* **NASA:** *page 8; map on pages 4-5:* **Nicoletta Ceresa**

Front cover: Clear, deep water and plentiful reef fish make the Elbow Reef's coral ridges a favorite dive site. (Photo: Stephen Frink/WaterHouse Stock Photography)

Text and photographs: Stephen Frink, William Harrigan
Text of "The Fish of the Florida Keys": Angelo Mojetta
Illustrators: Cristina Franco (dive sites) except "Spiegel Grove" by Claudio Nazzaro; Monica Falcone ("The Fish of the Florida Keys")
Copyeditor: John Kinsella, Diving Science and Technology Corp.
Production editor: Abigail Asher
Layout: Clara Zanotti
Text designers: Barbara Balch, Barbara Sturman
Jacket designer: Jordana Abrams

Second edition
10 9 8 7 6 5 4 3 2 1

ISBN 0-7892-0792-3
Library of Congress Cataloging-in-Publication Data available upon request

First Edition Library of Congress Cataloging-in-Publication Data
Frink, Stephen.
    [Florida Keys guida alle immersioni. English]
    The Florida Keys : text and photographs / by Stephen Frink and
William Harrigan ; editing provided by Diving Science and Technology
Corp. (DSAT).
        p.   cm. — (Abbeville dive guide)
    ISBN 0-7892-0394-4
    1. Scuba diving—Florida—Florida Keys—Guidebooks. 2. Florida
Keys (Fla.)—Guidebooks. I. Harrigan, William. II. Diving Science
and Technology Corp. III. Title. IV. Series.
    GV838.673.U6F75   1998
    917.59'41—dc21   97-41905